"FULL OF DIRECT HUMOR, HISTORICAL COMMENTARY, SENTIMENTAL BUT APT OBSERVATION."

— *THE CINCINNATI INQUIRER*

- Is a woman asking for trouble when she travels alone?

- Can housewives become exceptional people?

- What's wrong with the compulsory coupledom of marriage?

- Do singles live a glamorous or lonely lifestyle?

- Can three generations live under a single roof?

"A STIRRING AND ENLIGHTENING COLLECTION OF ESSAYS EXPLORING EXTRAORDINARY CHANGES IN THE LIVES OF ORDINARY WOMEN."

— *Publishers Weekly*

"JACOBY'S SHARP EYE AND CLEAR VOICE CAN PIERCE THE LATEST SHADOWS OF SEXUAL POLITICS."

— *Lois Gould*

THE
POSSIBLE
SHE

Susan Jacoby

BALLANTINE BOOKS • NEW YORK

All rights reserved. Published in the United States by Ballantine
Books, a division of Random House, Inc., New York, and
simultaneously in Canada by Random House of Canada, Limited,
Toronto, Canada.

Portions of this book first appeared, some in different form, in
The New York Times Magazine, McCall's, Working Woman,
and in a newsletter published by the Alicia Patterson Foundation under a grant from the Rockefeller Foundation

Acknowledgment is made to the publishers and authors for per-
mission to quote from the following: *A Bintel Brief* by Isaac
Metzker, translation copyright © 1971 by Isaac Metzker,
Doubleday & Company, Inc.; *The Breadgivers* by Anzia Yezierska, copyright 1925 by Doubleday & Company, Inc.; *World
of Our Fathers* by Irving Howe, copyright © 1976 by Irving
Howe, Harcourt Brace Jovanovich, Inc.; *The Woman Warrior:
Memoirs of a Girlhood Among Ghosts* by Maxine Hong Kingston, copyright © 1975, 1976 by Maxine Hong Kingston, Alfred
A. Knopf, Inc.; *The Fortunate Pilgrim* by Mario Puzo, copy-
right © 1964 by Mario Puzo, Candida Donadio & Associates,
Inc.; the collection of "Hers" articles by Susan Jacoby, copyright © 1977, 1978 by The New York Times Company

Library of Congress Catalog Card Number: 78-31830

ISBN 0-345-28735-5

This edition published by arrangement with Farrar, Straus
and Giroux

Manufactured in the United States of America

First Ballantine Books Edition: October 1980

To MANLEY AARON ASTRACHAN

MOST OF THESE ARTICLES appeared in magazines and newspapers between 1973 and 1978. In one form or another, all of them deal with the impact of feminism on the lives of women and on relations between women and men. The shorter essays in the collection—most of them included in the middle section of this book—were originally published as a series in the weekly "Hers" column of *The New York Times*. Those columns elicited a great many letters, and I have quoted from and commented on some of the more interesting ones.

The existence of this collection attests to the profound influence of feminism on my own life. I began working as a newspaper reporter at the age of seventeen, in 1963. At the time, I promised myself that I would never, never write about "women's subjects." To write about women was to write about trivia: charity balls, cake sales, and the like. Every ambitious young woman (and man) in my profession accepted the equation between women and trivia. I would have laughed at anyone who tried to tell me that one day I would believe the members of my own sex were important enough to write about.

Some readers will be bound to notice the absence of the title "Ms." in my writing, as well as the occasional presence of the titles "Mrs." and "Miss." In most nonfiction articles, I do not use honorifics for either women or men. It would be ludicrous to refer to the poet Anna Akhmatova as "Ms.," "Mrs.," or "Miss" Akhmatova. She is Akhmatova in second references, just as Boris Pasternak is Pasternak.

I always make exceptions to my style rules in order to follow the wishes of the people I write about. When "The Flatbush Feminists" was first published in *The New York Times,* the women were all adamant about wanting to be called "Mrs." —even though their names had been changed. Such desires should be respected, not only as a matter of courtesy, but in the interests of good writing. To call a woman "Ms." when she wants to be called "Mrs." (or "Mrs." when she wants to be called "Ms.") is to convey an inaccurate picture of the person she is. All the titles in this collection reflect the wishes of the subjects.

Most of the names of nonpublic figures have been changed at their request.

S.J.

New York, 1978

Contents

EXTRAORDINARY ORDINARY WOMEN

The Flatbush Feminists   3
A Letter to My Grandmother   17

MANNERS, MORALS, AND MONEY

Notes from a Free-Speech Junkie   29
Unfair Game   32
The First Girl at Second Base   39
Beyond the Ghetto   43
Kid Haters   46
What Does a Woman Want?   52
Wardrobe Engineering   56
Battering Back   59
Fear Taxes   63
The Single Life: Rich and Poor, Male and Female   66
The Great Couple-Friendship Fiction   79
Such Good Friends (Masculine Gender)   84
The Price of Pregnancy: Who Pays?   94
Old and Female: An Economic View   98
Getting Off the Dole   103
Three Generations, Two Women, One Roof   108
No Special Service—Just a Little Equality, Please   119

LOOKING BACK

Women of Letters   127
World of Our Mothers   131
We Did Overcome   142
The Education of a Feminist: Part One   151

Who ere she be,
That not impossible she
That shall command my heart and me . . .

—RICHARD CRASHAW

I know beginnings and endings
and life beyond death, and something else
I'd just as soon not think of now . . .
But if I could step outside myself
and contemplate the person that I am,
I would know at last what envy is.

—ANNA AKHMATOVA

EXTRAORDINARY ORDINARY WOMEN

The Flatbush Feminists

"I'M SHORT, FAT AND FORTY-FIVE."

Rose Danielli digs her fork into a large piece of Sara Lee cherry cheesecake as she begins to describe herself at the first meeting of a women's consciousness-raising group. Twelve women are crowded into the living room of a small red-brick house in the East Flatbush section of Brooklyn; many are old friends who have shared senior proms, weddings, births, miscarriages, family deaths, and all of the other minor and major events of life in a close-knit working-class community where neighbors still care about one another. Now they are supporting one another in a new experience: an effort to expand their middle-aged lives beyond the comfortable roles of wife, mother, and grandmother. No group of women seems further removed from the worlds of Gloria Steinem and Betty Friedan, *Ms.* magazine, marriage contracts, "alternative life styles," and all of the upper-middle-class paraphernalia frequently associated with the feminist movement. Nevertheless, the very existence of this group proves that the worlds are not as far apart as they seem.

"My mother-in-law asked me the other day if I was one of those 'women's libbers,'" continues Mrs. Danielli, "and I told her I had always been something of a 'libber' even though I like being called 'Mrs.' She said she guessed I was telling the truth, because she remembered how hard I fought for my girls to go to college. My husband and I never went to college, and everyone in the family thought our three girls would go to work to help put my son, Johnny, through. Way back when the kids were in grade school, I told my husband, 'Joe,

3

if one of our kids is going to college, all of them are going. Your girls aren't gonna have ten children like your mama—they've gotta do something with their lives just like our boy.'

"Both of our families were shocked when our oldest girl went off to college—Joe's papa kept asking if we didn't need the extra money she could bring in working as a typist. We needed money, all right, but I never gave in—even when times were toughest and we were eating spaghetti without meat sauce three nights a week."

There is a note of solid satisfaction in Rose Danielli's voice as she finishes both her story and the cheesecake. The women have agreed to begin their first session by describing the most significant failures and successes of their lives; they will start to talk about the future after evaluating the past. The old friendship and neighborly bonds give their discussion a more comfortable aura than the one that usually prevails in Manhattan consciousness-raising sessions, which frequently reflect the fragmented and transient nature of affluent high-rise apartment living.

"I was going to break the rules and interrupt," admits Alice Martino, a construction worker's wife who grew up on the same block with Rose in East Flatbush. "I thought Rose might go on and on about being fat, as though there were nothing more to her story."

The life stories outlined by the women have many common elements. The women are all in their forties; most grew up in first- and second-generation Italian or Jewish immigrant homes. A few have lived in East Flatbush since they were children, and the rest came from nearby blue-collar neighborhoods. Most of the women graduated from high school, went to work for a year or two at poorly paid jobs, married by age twenty, and quickly started having children. Only two of the twelve had any education beyond high school. Rose Danielli's background is typical; she worked as a telephone operator for a year before marrying Joe, a telephone installer, when they were both nineteen.

The husbands are blue-collar union men or white-collar workers employed by the city government; their income range is between $9,000 and $14,000 a year. Most of the families have at least three children. Homemade soups and clothes are a necessary economy for them rather than an expression of the "traditional female role." Their houses represent the only important financial investment of their lives and are maintained with appropriate care—postage-stamp lawns raked free of leaves, living-room sofas glazed with plastic slipcovers and reserved for company, starched kitchen curtains, home freezers stocked with the specials the women unearth in numerous grocery stores on Saturday mornings. They worry in equal measure about the rising price of ground chuck, the fact that so many of their grown children are leaving the old neighborhood, and how to get along with the blacks who are moving into the area. A dinner in a local Chinese or Italian restaurant is a once-a-month event. Manhattan is "the city," a place to be visited on wedding anniversaries for dinner and a hotel floor show.

Whatever their problems, the women love their husbands and are not about to leave them. They do not expect to liberate themselves by living alone, although they understand why some younger women find marriage an unsatisfactory state. They have neither the education nor the work experience to be tapped as token women for high-powered jobs in high-powered companies. One woman in the group says she is waiting breathlessly for the day when the local six o'clock news will feature a broadcaster who is not only black and female but over forty, thereby providing on-screen representation for three oppressed groups instead of two.

Nevertheless, the women are convinced that they can build a future different from the traditional path laid out by their mothers and grandmothers. The feminist movement is responsible in large measure for their belief that they can change the course of their middle-aged lives.

The movement was gaining strength and national publicity at a time when the women who make up the East Flatbush group began to face the void most full-time mothers experience after their children grow up and leave home. Their comments in the group sessions indicate that two main concerns spurred their interest in feminism: the feeling that society in general, and their husbands in particular, no longer viewed them as sexually interesting or even sexually functioning women, and the realization that they were "out of a job" in the same sense as a middle-aged man who is fired by his employer of twenty years.

The idea of a formal consciousness-raising group was suggested last fall by Lillian Schwartz, the only one of the women with any extensive contacts outside the neighborhood. She had been active for many years in citywide organizations concerned with the public schools, and she was hearing more and more about the feminist movement from the women she met in the course of her volunteer work. At the same time, her three closest friends in East Flatbush were constantly mulling over the question of what to do with the next twenty or thirty years of their lives. They agreed that an organized group might help them figure out what to do and quickly recruited enough interested women to make up a manageable dozen. Lillian hunted down a copy of *Ms.* with advice on how to form a consciousness-raising group.

The most important decision at the first meeting was that the sessions would be held regularly on Tuesday nights. Except in emergencies, they would not be subject to interference by children and husbands who had other activities in mind. At the second session, several women reported with glee that the announcement of a regular meeting had caused a storm in their homes. "In our house, my husband expects me home every evening," explained one woman. "That is, unless he decides to go bowling. Then I can go to the movies by myself or out to a neighbor's."

Some of the husbands resented the decision to regularize the meetings because they had chosen to view the group as just another *Kaffeeklatsch*. The reactions of the men included bitter opposition, secret sabotage, amused resignation, and quiet support. "My poor man asked what he should tell the neighbors if they called and asked for me on Tuesday night," recalled a woman whose husband is part owner of a Jewish delicatessen. "I told him to tell anyone who called the truth, that I'm working out what to do with my life. He said the hell he would, he'd tell them I was doing something for the temple."

Sarah Thomas, the forty-year-old wife of a policeman, had the biggest problem: Every time she planned to leave the house for her women's group, her husband had a minor household accident requiring her attention. The women were appropriately sympathetic when she arrived an hour late for the second meeting because her husband's ankle needed soaking after he twisted it on the front stoop. Before the next meeting, Sergeant Thomas carved a deep slice in his thumb with a potato peeler. When he poured boiling water over his hand, Sarah and the other women began to suspect the accidents were not entirely accidental.

At the fifth meeting, Sarah reported that "I told him since he was an experienced police officer he was used to dealing with emergencies and I was sure he could take care of a slight burn by himself. I figure if I just sail out of the house anyway, he'll stop having these accidents." (She proved a poor prophet, because she continued to attend the women's group meetings and, as of June, her husband was still chalking up at least two accidents a month.)

Most of the women spent considerable time talking about personal sexual problems during the early weeks of the group. In this respect, they resemble the younger wives, single women, and divorcées who make up the membership of most consciousness-raising groups. But they are of a more reserved and modest generation than the younger feminists. No one mentions foreplay or sexual positions. If the East Flatbush women are worried about orgasms, they do not talk about it. An occasional mention of premarital sex produces flushes of embarrassment. But they are all acutely aware of the unfulfilled sexual desires that seem to be the lot of many middle-aged women in American society. To a greater or lesser degree, most of the women reported the same problem: The frequency of sexual relations with their husbands diminished drastically after they entered their forties. For the unluckiest women, sex—like a night out in "the city"—became an event reserved for birthdays and anniversaries. "It's more like a monument than an act of love," one commented.

"I just want to be recognized as a woman," said Ruth Levine, a mother of five whose 100-pound figure and short black hair make her look a decade younger than her forty-six years. Her husband is a cab driver who has worked fourteen- to sixteen-hour days throughout most of their married life.

"I'm going to be alive for another twenty or thirty years," she observed. "My husband and I sleep together maybe once a month. Oh, it's not that he wants another woman—I don't think that at all. It's just that . . . I'm familiar. Men really don't think of women in their forties that way, in a sexual way. I know it isn't the way I look—I'm prettier now than I was when I had five children under the age of ten to run after all day. I don't feel like having orgies, but I'm too young for this . . . this . . . it's almost an end to sex. I don't know how to make my husband realize this without hurting him. I don't want him to feel I'm making demands he can't meet. And I don't even know if I have the courage to talk about it with him, after all these years of letting the man lead the way . . ."

Another woman sadly recalled a night when she put her arms around her husband while he was watching television and he pushed her away. "He said, 'Help, I married a sex maniac.' He made it sound like a joke, but I knew he was only half-teasing. Then he said, 'You know, Debbie, we're really getting too old for much fooling around. Our kids are going to be getting married pretty soon.' "

Alice Martino mocked the sex advice offered by conventional women's magazines. "They tell you to be careful to keep up your looks, don't walk around in front of your husband in rollers, go out and buy a new black negligée. But those little gems are stupid, because most women who like men have been following them for years. My hair is combed and my fanny is still pretty firm and I don't wear flannel pajamas to bed. It's the idea of settling into a new role after you get past a certain age that's so hard to fight.

"You know, when you were twenty the thing to do was make love and have children. Our eldest boy is getting married next month. The other night Rick said to me, 'Well, pretty soon I'll be able to call you Grandma.' I said he would over my dead body, that I would have murdered him if he'd called me 'Ma' while our kids were growing up. He laughed and said he was a fool, because he'd forgotten the time I shut him out of the bedroom after he gave me a new baby carriage for my birthday. A baby carriage. For *my* birthday!"

With the exception of Rose Danielli, who correctly surmised that losing sixty pounds would make a major change in her own sense of physical well-being as well as her husband's sexual behavior, the women agreed that spending money on "a new look" was not the answer to a lagging sex life. As a group, they were somewhat more tolerant of the sexual insecurities of middle-aged males than the younger women in consciousness-raising groups. Some of them compared the fatigue of their husbands with the exhaustion they felt when they were looking after small children.

"Life plays a dirty trick on women," said Ann Nussbaum, whose husband is a bookkeeper with the city Finance Administration. "The men think you're gorgeous when you're too young to know anything about life. How well I remember how hard it was to take any interest in my husband when I had been changing diapers all day. Now I have much more time and interest for sex, but my husband is the one who's beat. He does tax returns to make extra money on the side—I know he just feels like rolling over and going to sleep at the end of the day.

"One of the things I feel I have to get across to him is that being physically affectionate with each other doesn't have to mean sex; he doesn't have to feel all this pressure that men seem to feel about performance. I agree with Ruth that it's hard to talk about these things after a lifetime of being silent, but I don't see how we can get anywhere unless we speak up about what's bothering us."

As the group sessions continued, most of the women reported considerable success in their attempts to talk about sex with their husbands. They began seeking out more sex information from medical studies and books on women's health by feminist writers. Several women said their husbands were especially impressed by the Masters and Johnson finding that normal men and women can continue to enjoy sex into their sixties. Said Rose Danielli: "Joe told me, 'You know, Rose, we were brought up in ignorance even if we did manage to have four kids. This Masters-Johnson thing you're telling me about—I thought a wife would think her husband was a dirty old man if he kept trying to take her to bed when they were fifty years old."

One woman who was going through menopause reported that her husband was greatly relieved to learn she could still function sexually. "Like most of us here, I never really talked about these things with my husband. When I finally got up the nerve to say something, I found out he thought the change of life meant that a woman would find it difficult—physically difficult, that is—to have sex. I told him I was looking forward to the change because it meant I wouldn't have to worry about getting pregnant any more. He said he'd never looked at it that way."

Many members of the group linked their sexual plight with the more general emptiness of middle-aged women who have devoted their entire lives to their families. "My nights will take care of themselves if I have something to occupy my days," said one. By December—the third month of the group sessions—most of the discussions centered around the need to find some sort of work.

Ruth Levine, who had never worked outside her home, surprised the rest of the group by becoming the first to take the plunge into the job market. She applied for a job as a file clerk in a large advertising agency and was hired with a warning from the personnel department that "most of the girls on your floor will be twenty-five years younger than you are."

Feminist opponents of job discrimination are correct in their assertion that file clerking is a thankless, dead-end task reserved by large companies for women. However, the upper-middle-class, college-educated feminists often fail to realize that a woman with no training may look upon a mundane job as an opportunity rather than an insult. For Ruth Levine, who had rarely left her neighborhood for twenty-five years, the file clerk's job was an important step into a wider world.

"Well, I know it's not much of a job in the eyes of anyone else," she reported to her group after she had been working for a month. "Even the secretaries look down on file clerks—especially a file clerk in her forties. And I agree with some of the stuff I read in *Ms.* these days—a man, even a dumb one, would never have to take one of these jobs. But to me the job is something. Someone has to do this kind of work. I never went to college, I never worked before I was married, and I don't really have the training for anything more. What do I get out of the job? For one thing, I get to meet a lot of different people who give me new things to think about.

"The young girls ask me, 'Mrs. Levine, why are you working at your age when you have a husband and children? We're just waiting to get married and out of this hole.' I tell them I'm working because it's better than sitting home and being a vegetable, and that they should get themselves some more training or they'll be file clerks twenty years from now, whether they get married or not. I don't see any practical advice for girls like this in any of the magazines, including *Ms.* and *Cosmopolitan. Cosmo* tells girls how to put rouge on their breasts and *Ms.* tells you how to start your own business, but no one tells file clerks that life will stretch into a big zero unless they improve their skills."

The other important thing Ruth gets out of her job is money: She brings home more than $90 a week after taxes and Social Security withholding. "It makes me feel both that I'm independent and that I'm contributing something to the household," she said.

Sarah, the wife of the accident-prone police sergeant, broke in: "Whenever I talk about getting a job, my husband says I'm contributing something by staying home and taking care of the house."

"I know, I know, I've heard it all," Ruth replied. "My Hal said exactly the same thing. He said it made him feel like a second-class man, that he couldn't take care of his family by himself. I said, 'Hal, our youngest kid is sixteen. What am I going to do with myself for the next twenty years?' I told him I'd feel like we were pulling together—the way we did when the kids were little—if I could bring in a little money to make our lives easier.

"At first we agreed the money would go into a special account in my name, so it would be clear he was still paying for everything. Finally Hal saw the money was piling up and it was crazy not to use it. We put part of it into the regular budget and are saving the rest for a vacation."

Ruth reported that her husband's attitude toward her job changed slowly but definitely. He became less concerned about the fact that she was making money of her own and began to cut down on his own fourteen-hour work days in his taxi. The most unexpected dividend was a significant improvement in their sex life.

"I can't believe it. We have a sex life again. For the first time in years Hal can go out with me once a week; he comes home at seven o'clock instead of midnight. That little bit of extra money makes a big difference to us. We go to bed together more than we did for the last ten years.

"Hal and I have never been much for talking about sex, but one night he turned to me in bed and said, 'You know, Ruthie, I was just too beat to pay attention to you this way. I didn't realize it until you went to work and took some of the money pressure off me.' I said, 'You know, Hal, I didn't realize it either.' "

Ruth is taking a shorthand course so that she can move into a better-paying secretarial job next fall. After she took the first step, four other women in the group found jobs. Two returned to the secretarial work they had done before they were married, one found an opening as a teacher aide in the Head Start program for preschool children, and another put her fluent Italian to work as an interpreter for older immigrants in their dealing with city agencies. Two women in the group decided they would go to college and were accepted in adult-education programs leading toward a bachelor's degree.

The women who plan to enter college are undergoing profound changes that have also made a deep impact on their husbands. "I don't think I could take file clerking," announced Alice Martino one night, "but I'm not prepared for anything else. I always wanted to go to college, and I think that's just what I'm going to do."

Unlike many of the women, Alice has no serious financial problems. Her husband, Rick, earns more than $16,000 a year as a construction worker; they live rent-and-mortgage-free in a house Alice's mother left them when she died. Their children are between ages eighteen and twenty-four, and are either currently attending college or have graduated.

Alice is enrolling in the highly respected adult-education program at Brooklyn College. After considering several possibilities, she decided on teaching as a career because she felt it offered the easiest entree for an older woman. She plans to make a specialty of speech and reading therapy because there is a shortage of trained personnel in those areas despite an overall teacher surplus.

Contradicting the hard-hat stereotype, Alice's husband turned out to be more favorably disposed toward the feminist movement than the other women's husbands. In fact, he decided to follow his wife's example. "He confessed he was jealous of my plans to go to college," Alice said, "and then he decided he was being stupid because he could do it too. College was never a possibility for him when he was younger—he was the oldest son and his parents needed money very badly. He's thought about architectural engineering for years;

he always said he knew more about putting up buildings than the engineers on the job.

"Anyway, he said he always assumed a man couldn't change his life in midstream, but he figured if women were trying to do it, why not him. It won't be easy for him trying to build a new career when he's over forty, but it won't be easy for me either. We have it planned. I'll be teaching before Rick gets his engineering degree, and he'll have a pension because he's been in the union since he was eighteen. We'll have plenty of money to get along on while he looks for an employer who doesn't think a man is a fossil when he gets to be forty. As far as my teaching goes, I'll be less of a fossil than the younger teachers."

One of the more conservative women in the group told Alice she sounded like a starry-eyed eighteen-year-old. "I feel like one," she replied. "I haven't been this optimistic about life since I was eighteen."

Joan Loewenstein, who is also entering Brooklyn College next fall, was equally optimistic. She hopes to become a statistician or a computer programmer. "A lot of people have been telling me I'm out of my mind to be thinking about this big a change 'at your age.' Oh, they love to use that phrase—'at your age.' But I've been lucky like Alice—my husband has been wonderful. His partner in the deli started this business about my age, and he said, 'What do you think she should do at her age, buy a cemetery plot?' Abe is convinced I have a talent for math because I've always helped him keep the books for the store, done our income-tax return, that sort of thing.

"You know, we had a joint checking account all of our lives, but Abe always gave me the household money every week. I never wrote a check for anything unless it was something like the mortgage payment. I would never have bought myself a new dress without checking with him first. Abe has been doing some thinking on his own about women's lib. He says it suddenly hit him how stupid it was for him to be doling out household money to me when I keep the books better than he does.

"So the other night he tells me, 'Joan, I'm not giving you money for the house any more; you take what you need. Here I am, a man who's been letting a woman keep his books for twenty years, and still telling her what to spend each week. I know what I got out of it, but what did you get? I never really wanted to be cheap, it was just the way my parents did things.'

"You know, I was surprised at all this from Abe. Then I started thinking about that question—what *did* I get out of it. Well, I told Abe I was able to save some money from my allowance on the sly. He said, 'So, now you'll save on the open.' I guess it was sort of comfortable, acting like a little girl about money. Anyway, it sure won't do for a college girl—oops, woman—who wants to program computers."

Not all the women have had as much success in changing their own lives or the attitudes of their husbands. Judith Katz, who worked as a secretary before her marriage twenty years ago, encountered stiff opposition when she went back to work in the counseling office of a Brooklyn junior high school. Her husband especially resents the fact that she wanted a job enough to take an opening in a ghetto school with a tough reputation. As an expression of his disapproval, he refuses to ride the subway with his wife in the morning. Another of the women, an accountant's wife who is already attending classes at Brooklyn College, did not speak to her husband for several weeks after he told her, "You're too featherbrained to finish cleaning the house, much less four years of college."

In general, the East Flatbush men who disapprove of feminism express their reactions more openly than the professional husbands of upper-middle-class women who are the most vocal and visible participants in the movement. College-educated men are often reluctant to attack women's liberation in principle, but their practical behavior is another matter. Judging from the wide variety of male reactions described by the Flatbush wives, blue-collar men are no more or no less disturbed than other American men when the women in their lives try to break out of the traditional female pattern.

The East Flatbush women have considerable difficulty identifying with the widely publicized leaders of the movement. Said one: "I confess I don't feel much of a sense of sisterhood when I see pictures of Gloria Steinem with her streaked hair and slinky figure. I feel somehow that these people don't know how it is to be getting older with very little money and education. They have it a lot better than we do—it's not true that we're all in the same boat."

Another woman disagreed: "Well, there's one thing we all have in common—we're all afraid of muggers and rapists when we walk down a dark street at night. And that's something we have in common with the colored women who live right here in East Flatbush, even though most of us are better off financially than they are."

The women do identify with the movement on a variety of specific issues—day-care centers, equal pay for equal work, the right to abortion and contraceptive information, the need to educate young girls to think of themselves as individuals in their own right instead of viewing themselves only as future wives and mothers. Several of the women now spend considerable time trying to introduce these ideas into the conservative social environment of East Flatbush. One of their immediate goals is a health information service for girls and women of all ages; they feel that most East Flatbush women are unlikely to use the referral services now available in Manhattan. Rose Danielli had hoped to organize such a service through her church but ran headon into a clash with her priest over contraceptive information.

"My husband said, 'Oh, Rose, don't get into a battle with Father———.' Then he said, 'I give up. If you were willing to do battle with my mama you won't stop with the priest.'

"But Joe doesn't really mind the way I feel—in fact, I think he's kind of proud. This year our oldest girl gets her doctor's degree from Stanford, our boy gets his master's, and our second youngest girl graduates from Hunter College. Joe told his parents the other night that sending all of his kids through college was the proudest accomplishment of his life, and that he wouldn't have done it if I hadn't insisted.

"We had to fight our girls, too, until they were old enough to have some sense. They used to remind me that I got married when I was nineteen and their dad and I were happy. I just told them their grandparents never finished high school and they were happy too, but it's not progress if the next generation lives the same way. To me, that's what women's lib is all about—progress. In small steps, maybe, but still progress."

Next fall, the East Flatbush group will take in five new women because several of the founding members will be too busy with jobs and college courses. All of the women call that progress.

—*June 1973*

A Letter to My Grandmother

DEAR GRANNY,

Ever since Gramps died, I have thought more and more about the important role the two of you have played in my life. I too am growing older: At thirty-two, I am much more aware than I was in my twenties of the ways in which I have been shaped by the past. Not my own self-centered past, the one that begins with a memory flash of your coming to take care of me while my mother goes off to the hospital to have a baby (*Whose baby? What can it have to do with me?*), but the past represented by generations of relatives who came before me.

There you are, you see, in my first conscious memory. My mother left me—I don't remember her leaving me before then, though she surely must have done so—and came home with a baby brother. My parents brought Robbie home to your old house with the wonderful attic, not to our small apartment in the city. I suppose I must have been jealous, but I don't remember that either. I do remember your talking to me before they came home and telling me I would always be special because I was the *first* grandchild.

I remember something else even more vividly. Not too long after my brother was born, my mother went back to the hospital for several weeks. I was so scared, because I knew that being sick in the hospital was not the same as going to the hospital to have a baby. I don't know whether I overheard the words "breast abscess" then or whether I learned much later why my mother had left me again. I do know that the same terror gripped me twenty-four years later, when I phoned my mother to hear the news that the unimportant lump in her breast had turned out to be cancer and that she had just undergone a radical mastectomy. For weeks afterward, I would wake up in an icy sweat night after night. Then you came to me in a dream, in the bedroom where I used to sleep under the eaves of your house. (*Everything's going to be all right, Susie. Your mamma wouldn't leave you, any more than I would leave her. She'll be home soon. I'll stay here till you fall asleep.*) When I woke up in my New York apartment, your soothing chant—the one you must have comforted me with when I was only three—was still with me. *Your mamma wouldn't leave you, any more than I would leave her.* Those nightmare sweats haven't come back.

I feel sorry for people my age who never really knew their grandparents. Growing up in the fifties deprived many of us of the family ties that previous generations of Americans took for granted. I was lucky. For the first eight years of my life we lived just a few minutes away from each other. Later, when my family moved from Chicago to Michigan, I spent a large chunk of every summer vacation with you.

I adored Gramps just as I adored you, but my memories of him focus mainly on "special occasions"—holidays, birthdays, a lunch in the Loop when he took me to a restaurant with the first French pastry tray I had ever seen, my first baseball game in Comiskey Park. You were the one in charge of everyday life, and you exerted a constant and loving influence on my idea and, in some respects, my ideal of what it means to be a woman.

I often start thinking about you when I am standing next to a kitchen stove. Like you (and unlike my mother), I love to cook. I inherited many of my favorite recipes from you. I understand exactly why I know how to fix potatoes twenty different ways and why my health-food-freak friends are horrified at the starch and calorie content of my meals. You were the daughter of German immigrants, and you found it hard to imagine a meal without potatoes. I too feel a growl of protest in my stomach when I confront a meal without potatoes—that is, unless there is some pasta in sight. I understand the potatoes, but I can't quite figure out how your German heritage taught you to make such terrific spaghetti sauce. I make mine just the way you did, simmering it for hours with lots of fresh garlic and onions and tomatoes and bay leaves. I've been to Italy six times in the last ten years, Gran, and there isn't any better sauce than yours. The meatballs I make with fresh beef and pork, ground by the butcher right in front of my eyes. *Never buy any chopped meat unless you've seen what went into the grinder, Susie.* I never do. In the supermarket I am amazed at the women who seem perfectly content to pick up plastic-wrapped packages of what is supposed to be meat. Didn't they have grandmothers to tell them anything?

Like you, I consider food an important expression of love, friendship, and hospitality. I loathe the all-American custom of cementing business relationships by having people over to eat. I do business in restaurants. In my home I feed only my real friends. Apart from making love, there's nothing I like to do more with a man I love than to cook for him.

I know the equation between food and love can be overdone. Since my mother and I have both grown up enough to talk about *her* childhood, I have learned that she was once fat and blames you for stuffing her when she was little. That's the difference between being a parent and a grandparent. A grandmother can stuff a grandchild with food and love without the awful weight of responsibility that makes a parent the target of old childhood fears and resentments—even though the parent may be seventy and the child fifty. The relationship between a grandparent and a grandchild offers one of the few opportunities for people to give and receive unquestioning, undemanding love.

Granny, I don't want you to think all this talk about food means I picture you as a pink-cheeked, white-haired Norman Rockwell grandmother. The things we talked about while I was growing up were infinitely more important than the food you served. One of the most important things I learned from you was that the affluence and, more significantly, the expectation of ever-increasing affluence that surrounded me in the late 1950's were not part of the natural order of the universe but were, in fact, a departure from the more modest hopes of previous generations. Hard physical work—not dancing lessons and college catalogues—was the reality of your youth. You came from a large family, and you found your first job pulling up onions for a nickel a bushel. I was always fascinated by that true story, because you never failed to point out that the fields where you once worked lay beneath the very pavement that was turning the countryside around Chicago into an endless suburb.

You told me how much you wanted to finish high school and how you were prevented from graduating because you had to help support your brothers and sisters after your stepfather died. When you were sixteen, you quit school and went to work as a comptometer operator. I know you didn't think about it at the time, but you were a member of the first generation of young American women who were able to earn a living through office work rather than through the most menial factory jobs. I don't think you were especially proud of the fact that you helped your mother feed your family; it never would have occurred to you to place your personal desires above your duty. Just before I graduated from high school, you told me how proud you were of me and how you had always felt inferior to other people because you never got your diploma. How I wish I had told you then that *I* was proud of *you*. But I felt like the smartest kid on the block (hadn't I won three scholarships? Wasn't I already working on a college newspaper while I was still in high school?) and, to tell the truth, I shared your feelings about your lack of formal education. I was really proud of myself back in 1963. There I was, writing spirited columns in defense of the rights of Negroes ("black" was not yet considered a beautiful word), and it was painfully embarrassing to me to hear you call them "the colored." *How can she be so insensitive; age is no excuse.*

Now I remember just what it was you told me about "the colored" when I was a child. The parochial school I attended was located in a working-class neighborhood, populated mainly by whites of Irish and Polish descent. "The colored," pushing out from Chicago, were beginning to move in and already arousing resentment. *Susie, the color of a person's skin is not what's really important. It's what's inside that counts, what's in the heart. There are good and bad colored, just like there are good and bad white people.* This after I reported a fight between a black boy and a white boy on the playground that day. Do you remember? Could anyone with a college education have told me anything more useful or more true about the differences between black and white?

I write a good deal these days about the problems of "the aging," as I once wrote about "civil rights." Only I don't write with the certainty and righteousness of my youth. Thanks to you, I know exactly what I should do about "the aging" in my own life. If my parents ever need my help, I should take care of them as you took care of your mother and as my mother will take care of you. Thanks to the selfishness and drive that have made me a writer, I know that what I should do and what I will do are probably two different things.

My great-grandmother, who was called Howdy because that's how she always greeted children, lived with you when I was a little girl and she was in her eighties. When I was very young, it seemed to me that Howdy talked and moved like everyone else, the only difference being that her hair was whiter. By the time I was eight or nine, I realized Howdy could no longer do much for herself and her conversation didn't make much sense. I remember your brushing out her long, thick hair. I also remember your changing soiled sheets and helping her to the bathroom when she could no longer control her bodily functions.

Is everybody like that when they get old, Granny? Why can't Howdy go to the bathroom by herself?

When I was a little girl, my mother took care of me. Now it's my turn to take care of her.

But is everybody old like that?

Go play with your Gramps' poker chips, Susie. I'll be done in a minute.

As Howdy aged, she muttered more and more to herself in her native German. Long after her death, you told me my great-grandmother had been quite an adventurer in her youth. When she was only fifteen, she ran away from Stuttgart with a girlfriend and made the long trip across the ocean in steerage to the United States. I'm happy to know I am descended from an intrepid woman. I'm grateful you gave me the opportunity to know and remember Howdy.

People can talk all they want about the tensions that used to exist in three-generation households. I don't remember tension in your home. Yes, I know the peace was maintained by immense self-sacrifice on your part: You did all the work. I don't live in a sprawling house but in a city apartment that barely has room for my husband and me, much less for anyone else. I live a thousand miles from my parents. Even if they lived in New York, the demands of my work would make it impossible for me to take care of them the way you took care of Howdy. They would hate living with me as much as I would hate living with them. But these rationalizations stick in my throat. In my heart, I believe that yours was a better and more human way of treating "the aging." There must be some compromise between my own needs and the sheer neglect represented by "planned retirement communities."

I haven't seen as much of you as I should have, or as I would have liked to, since I moved away from the Midwest. I am especially grateful for something you did for your "grown-up" granddaughter at a particularly difficult point in her life. You probably don't remember what it was, since it was only one in a long string of gifts you bestowed on me.

I had just turned twenty and was mired in a senseless, too-early marriage that had reduced me to such inarticulate misery and my parents to such articulate fury that communication between us had ceased. I was also poor and had to borrow money from a professor for the air fare to go East for a job interview with *The Washington Post*. The *Post* gave me the job as a reporter, but that did not solve my marital or financial problems. During the summer, when I was finishing college and preparing to move to Washington, I visited you for a few days. You didn't give me any lectures about the marriage. Instead, you asked me if I had any clothes to wear on my new job. I was worried about that; I had no adult-looking clothes and no hope of scraping up enough money to buy some. You took me to Bonwit Teller (yes, I had stopped scorning bourgeois comforts after doing without them for two years) and told me to pick out any dress I wanted. I remember every detail of that dress: a sleeveless, bright-pink wool A-line with a matching jacket, of the kind popularized by Jackie Kennedy in the early sixties. I wore that dress a lot; it was the only new piece of clothing I was to own until I crawled out from under a pile of postcollege and postmarital debts.

I couldn't possibly pay you back for everything you

have meant to me and done for me—I know you never expected that from me—but at least I was able to do something for you after Gramps died. Do you remember the night I spent with you when I was able to stop over in Chicago on a magazine assignment? We talked about Gramps far into the night—what he looked like as a young man, how you and he felt when you had an unexpected second child fourteen years after my mother was born, how you wore a pastel dress at his funeral because he hated women in black, how lonely you had been since his death, how pleased you were that you could keep your finances in order. You told me it was easier to talk about your memories with me than with my mother, because my mother had so idolized her father that it was more painful for her to think about him than for you. And you didn't want to cause my mother pain. *So what's a granddaughter for?* Pleased, at last, to be paying back a little of my debt to you.

My memories of you are responsible for vast areas of ambivalence in my mind and soul. I know I am incapable of devoting myself to the needs of others as you did—and I don't really want to live my life that way—but I wonder if I would be as strong as I am without the experience of your devotion. I don't wonder about you. I realize you may not have been the perfect mother to your own children—what mother is?—but you were a perfect grandmother to me. The Book of Proverbs (31: 25-31) says it better than I ever could:

"Strength and honor are her clothing; and she shall rejoice in time to come.

"She openeth her mouth with wisdom; and in her tongue is the law of kindness.

"She looketh well to the ways of her household, and eateth not the bread of idleness.

"Her children arise up, and call her blessed; her husband also, and he praiseth her.

"Many daughters have done virtuously, but thou excellest them all.

"Favor is deceitful, and beauty is vain: but a woman that feareth the Lord, she shall be praised.

"Give her of the fruit of her hands; and let her own works praise her in the gates."

Much love,
SUSAN

—October 1977

MANNERS, MORALS, AND MONEY

Notes from a Free-Speech Junkie

IT IS NO NEWS that many women are defecting from the ranks of civil libertarians on the issue of obscenity. The conviction of Larry Flynt, publisher of *Hustler* magazine—before his metamorphosis into a born-again Christian—was greeted with unabashed feminist approval. Harry Reems, the unknown actor who was convicted by a Memphis jury for conspiring to distribute the movie *Deep Throat,* has carried on his legal battles with almost no help from women who ordinarily regard themselves as supporters of the First Amendment. Feminist writers and scholars have even discussed the possibility of making common cause against pornography with adversaries of the women's movement—including opponents of the Equal Rights Amendment and "right to life" forces.

All of this is deeply disturbing to a woman who believes, as I always have and still do, in an absolute interpretation of the First Amendment. Nothing in Larry Flynt's garbage convinces me that the late Justice Hugo L. Black was wrong in his opinion that "the Federal government is without any power whatsoever under the Constitution to put any type of burden on free speech and expression of ideas of any kind (as distinguished from conduct)." Many women I like and respect tell me I am wrong; I cannot remember having become involved in so many heated discussions of a public issue since the end of the Vietnam war. A feminist writer described my views as those of a "First Amendment junkie."

Many feminist arguments for controls on pornography carry the implicit conviction that porn books, magazines, and movies pose a greater threat to women than similarly repulsive exercises of free speech pose to other offended groups. This conviction has, of course, been shared by everyone—regardless of race, creed, or sex—who has ever argued in favor of abridging the First Amendment. It is the argument used by some Jews who have withdrawn their support from the American Civil Liberties Union because it has defended the right of American Nazis to march through a community inhabited by survivors of Hitler's concentration camps.

If feminists want to argue that the protection of the Constitution should not be extended to *any* particularly odious or threatening form of speech, they have a reasonable argument (although I don't agree with it). But it is ridiculous to suggest that the porn shops in Times Square are more disgusting to women than a march of neo-Nazis is to survivors of the extermination camps.

The arguments over pornography also blur the vital distinction between expression of ideas and conduct. When I say I believe unreservedly in the First Amendment, someone always comes back at me with the issue of "kiddie porn." But kiddie porn is not a First Amendment issue. It is an issue of the abuse of power—the power adults have over children—and not of obscenity. Parents and promoters have no more right to use their children to make porn movies than they do to send them to work in coal mines. The responsible adults should be prosecuted, just as adults who use children for backbreaking farm labor should be prosecuted.

Susan Brownmiller, in *Against Our Will: Men, Women and Rape*, has described pornography as "the undiluted essence of anti-female propaganda." I think this is a fair description of some types of pornography, especially of the brutish subspecies that equates sex with death and portrays women primarily as objects of violence.

The equation of sex and violence, personified by some glossy rock record album covers as well as by *Hustler,* has fed the illusion that censorship of pornography can be conducted on a more rational basis than other types of censorship. Are all pictures of naked women obscene? Clearly not, says a friend. A Renoir nude is art, she says, and *Hustler* is trash. "Any reasonable person" knows that.

But what about something between art and trash—something, say, along the lines of *Playboy* or *Penthouse* magazines? I asked five women for their reactions to one picture in *Penthouse* and got responses that ranged from "lovely" and "sensuous" to "revolting" and "demeaning." Feminists, like everyone else, seldom have rational reasons for their preferences in erotica. Like members of juries, they tend to disagree when confronted with something that falls short of 100 per cent vulgarity.

In any case, feminists will not be the arbiters of good taste if it becomes easier to harass, prosecute, and convict people on obscenity charges. Most of the people who want to censor girlie magazines are equally opposed to open discussion of issues that are of vital concern to women: rape, abortion, menstruation, contraception, lesbianism—in fact, the entire range of sexual experience from a woman's viewpoint.

Feminist writers and editors and filmmakers have limited financial resources: Confronted by a determined prosecutor, Hugh Hefner will fare better than Susan Brownmiller. Would the Memphis jurors who convicted Harry Reems for his role in *Deep Throat* be inclined to take a more positive view of paintings of the female genitalia done by sensitive feminist artists? *Ms.* magazine has printed color reproductions of some of those art works; *Ms.* is already banned from a number of high school libraries because someone considers it threatening and/or obscene.

Feminists who want to censor what they regard as harmful pornography have essentially the same motivation as other would-be censors: They want to use the power of the state to accomplish what they have been unable to achieve in the marketplace of ideas and images. The impulse to censor places no faith in the possibilities of democratic persuasion.

It isn't easy to persuade certain men that they have better uses for $1.95 each month than to spend it on a copy of *Hustler?* Well, then, give the men no choice in the matter.

I believe there is also a connection between the impulse toward censorship on the part of people who used to consider themselves civil libertarians and a more general desire to shift responsibility from individuals to institutions. When I saw the movie *Looking for Mr. Goodbar,* I was stunned by its series of visual images equating sex and violence, coupled with what seems to me the mindless message (a distortion of the fine Judith Rossner novel) that casual sex equals death. When I came out of the movie, I was even more shocked to see parents standing in line with children between the ages of ten and fourteen.

I simply don't know why a parent would take a child to see such a movie, any more than I understand why people feel they can't turn off a television set their child is watching. Whenever I say that, my friends tell me I don't know how it is because I don't have children. True, but I do have parents. When I was a child, they did turn off the TV. They didn't expect the Federal Communications Commission to do their job for them.

I am a First Amendment junkie. You can't OD on the First Amendment, because free speech is its own best antidote.

—January 1978

Unfair Game

MY FRIEND AND I, two women obviously engrossed in conversation, are sitting at a corner table in the crowded Oak Room of the Plaza at ten o'clock on a Tuesday night. A man materializes and interrupts us with the snappy opening line, "A good woman is hard to find."

We say nothing, hoping he will disappear back into his bottle. But he fancies himself as our genie and asks, "Are you visiting?" Still we say nothing. Finally my friend looks up and says, "We live here." She and I look at each other, the thread of our conversation snapped, our thoughts focused on how to get rid of the intruder. In a minute, if something isn't done, he will scrunch down next to me on the banquette and start offering to buy us drinks.

"Would you leave us alone, please," I say in a loud but reasonably polite voice. He looks slightly offended but goes on with his bright social patter. I become more explicit. "We don't want to talk to you, we didn't ask you over here, and we want to be alone. Go away." This time he directs his full attention to me—and he is mad. "All right, all right, *excuse me*." He pushes up the corners of his mouth in a Howdy Doody smile. "You ought to try smiling. You might even be pretty if you smiled once in a while."

At last the man leaves. He goes back to his buddy at the bar. I watch them out of the corner of my eye, and he gestures angrily at me for at least fifteen minutes. When he passes our table on the way out of the room, this well-dressed, obviously affluent man mutters, "Good-bye, bitch," under his breath.

Why is this man calling me names? Because I have asserted my right to sit at a table in a public place without being drawn into a sexual flirtation. Because he has been told, in no uncertain terms, that two attractive women prefer each other's company to his.

This sort of experience is an old story to any woman who travels, eats, or drinks—for business or pleasure—without a male escort. In Holiday Inns and at the Plaza, on buses and airplanes, in tourist and first class, a woman is always thought to be looking for a man in addition to whatever else she may be doing. The man who barged in on us at the bar would never have broken into the conversation of two men, and it goes without saying that he wouldn't have imposed himself on a man and a woman who were having a drink. But two women at a table are an entirely different matter. Fair game.

This might be viewed as a relatively small flaw in the order of the universe—something in a class with an airline losing luggage or a computer fouling up a bank statement. Except a computer doesn't foul up your bank account every month and an airline doesn't lose your suitcase every time you fly. But if you are an independent woman, you have to spend a certain amount of energy, day in and day out, in order to go about your business without being bothered by strange men.

On airplanes, I am a close-mouthed traveler. As soon as the "No Smoking" sign is turned off, I usually pull some papers out of my briefcase and start working. Work helps me forget that I am scared of flying. When I am sitting next to a woman, she quickly realizes from my monosyllabic replies that I don't want to chat during the flight. Most men, though, are not content to be ignored.

Once I was flying from New York to San Antonio on a plane that was scheduled to stop in Dallas. My seatmate was an advertising executive who kept questioning me about what I was doing and who remained undiscouraged by my terse replies until I ostentatiously covered myself with a blanket and shut my eyes. When the plane started its descent into Dallas, he made his move.

"You don't really have to get to San Antonio today, do you?"

"Yes."

"Come on, change your ticket. Spend the evening with me here. I'm staying at a wonderful hotel, with a pool, we could go dancing . . ."

"No."

"Well, you can't blame a man for trying."

I do blame a man for trying in this situation—for suggesting that a woman change her work and travel plans to spend a night with a perfect stranger in whom she had displayed no personal interest. The "no personal interest" is crucial; I wouldn't have blamed the man for trying if I had been stroking his cheek and complaining about my dull social life.

There is a nice postscript to this story. Several months later, I was walking my dog in Carl Schurz Park when I ran into my erstwhile seatmate, who was taking a stroll with his wife and children. He recognized me, all right, and was trying to avoid me when I went over and courteously reintroduced myself. I reminded him that we had been on the same flight to Dallas. "Oh yes," he said. "As I recall you were going on to somewhere else." "San Antonio," I said. "I was in a hurry that day."

The code of feminine politeness, instilled in girlhood, is no help in dealing with the unwanted approaches of strange men. Our mothers didn't teach us to tell a man to get lost; they told us to smile and hint that we'd be just delighted to spend time with the gentleman if we didn't have other commitments. The man in the Oak Room bar would not be put off by a demure lowering of eyelids; he had to be told, roughly and loudly, that his presence was a nuisance.

Not that I am necessarily against men and women picking each other up in public places. In most instances, a modicum of sensitivity will tell a woman or a man whether someone is open to approaches.

Mistakes can easily be corrected by the kind of courtesy so many people have abandoned since the "sexual revolution." One summer evening, I was whiling away a half hour in the outdoor bar of the Stanhope Hotel. I was alone, dressed up, having a drink before going on to meet someone in a restaurant. A man at the next table asked, "If you're not busy, would you like to have a drink with me?" I told him I was sorry but I would be leaving shortly. "Excuse me for disturbing you," he said, turning back to his own drink. Simple courtesy. No insults and no hurt feelings.

One friend suggested that I might have avoided the incident in the Oak Room by going to the Palm Court instead. It's true that the Palm Court is a traditional meeting place for unescorted ladies. But I don't like violins when I want to talk. And I wanted to sit in a large, comfortable leather chair. Why should I have to hide among the potted palms to avoid men who think I'm looking for something else?

—February 1978

The above column, which appeared in *The New York Times*, drew a larger response than anything I have published in my fifteen years as a newspaper and magazine writer. Within two weeks, I had received eighty-two letters—twenty-nine from women, fifty-three from men. This is also the only article I have ever written that elicited a response dramatically divided along sex lines. The women (with a few exceptions) said, "Yes, that's just how it is. I'm going to pin your column on the bulletin board at the office so the men can read it." The men (again, with a few exceptions) revealed a mean underside that is usually veiled in public social exchanges between the sexes. Their letters offered the following interpretations of my behavior:

1. I was an Ugly Duckling who was working out my pathetic fantasies that men found me attractive. This viewpoint was summed up most succinctly by C. H. "Max" Freedman, publisher of a unique little sheet called *Talknews*. He noted that "a while back on these pages I characterized someone as stirring men's imaginations 'about as much as an over-fried *latke*.' But I wouldn't go nearly this far with you, Jacoby. Of course you too could be described as having all the attraction of said *latke*—but in your case only after it's been digested."

2. I was a Beautiful Temptress who made it impossible for any red-blooded man to leave me alone. (Sometimes, the Beautiful Temptress theory and the Ugly Duckling theory appeared in the same letter.)

3. My presence without a male escort in a bar or restaurant constituted *prima facie* evidence that I was "asking for it."

4. Even if I wasn't "asking for it," I should certainly sympathize with men who are unable to distinguish me

from all those other women who are "asking for it." As one man wrote, "If Miss Jacoby expects the male to know one sister from another—please! Perhaps today's woman should wear some sort of a forehead stamp: Lady, bar person, prostitute, etc., then Miss Jacoby would have a reason to complain if she was wrongfully approached."

A nice touch, that forehead stamp. The same argument was advanced in one form or another by most of my male correspondents: How can a man be expected to tell a "lady" from a "swinger" or a "prostitute"? How indeed, in the absence of the rational presumption that a woman, like a man, is simply a human being who wants to go about her own business?

One man, referring to the incident on the plane, asked, "Why is a man obliged to recognize a woman for what she (in her mind) is? Women have opened the door for these traveling Romeos. There is a whole class of women who welcome the advances of the married man, so that in fact the traveling Romeo usually makes his marital status known as quickly as possible. His wedding ring is an asset!"

Another man took me to task for failing to understand the sensitive male ego. "Men and women dance around each other, send cryptic messages, and sometimes play devious games. I don't deny that there are many men who come on like Hamilton Jordan, but there are more who might be mesmerized by the prospect of meeting you and/or your friend and choked by their own self-consciousness into seeming more like mashers than they really are. It is difficult for a man to imagine a woman could be insensitive to this. In fact, we tend to assume that women play on our compulsions. When they attract us and reject us, it is hard not to think of them as 'bitches.' "

There it is: Simply by spending an hour in a bar with a female friend, a woman is playing on a man's compulsions, attracting him, rejecting him, and meriting the label of "bitch." If I were to suggest that two men at a nearby table were "attracting" or "rejecting" me simply because they wanted to conduct an uninterrupted conversation, I would, correctly, be regarded as demented.

Several men asked why I had made a point of meeting a "girlfriend" in a bar at night if I was really serious about not wanting to socialize with men. It never occurred to them that my friend and I might have wanted a quiet drink on the way home after a hard day, as countless men do in similar situations. We had, in fact, just left a meeting of a professional organization. The Plaza offered the nearest bar with a relatively quiet atmosphere and comfortable chairs. It is interesting that all of my correspondents chose to picture me as a woman spending a gay night on the town.

One man, in a lengthy letter, did express sympathy and understanding for women who are subjected to unwanted intrusions. His understanding flowed from personal exposure to the sort of treatment that is rarely experienced by heterosexual men.

"I find myself in complete agreement," he wrote, "that if a man is not receiving some sort of positive response from a woman, he should back off and not continue his actions to the point of harassment. As a bachelor, I am aware of the necessity of personally being aggressive but also of knowing when a particular approach will be fruitless.

"My reason for writing is to elaborate on the theme of your column. Men too can be harassed by people who envision themselves as being well-intentioned. In my case, this does not take the form of sexual advances but rather of loud comments. I stand 6 feet, 7½ inches tall, and easily hide some 245 pounds on a moderately athletic build. I cause a stir when I walk into a roomful of strangers, for I am not 'everyman.'

"I try to graciously tolerate the inane comments such as 'How's the weather up there?' or 'Hiya, Shorty!' Then, there are men who will consider a person of my size as being fair game, and these people are particularly hard to shake off. The worst type consists of the fellow who is not of my stature but wants to take on the biggest guy in the bar. The second case is the person who will not believe I do not play basketball. He then proceeds to say loudly that I would have 'made it' if I had played the game.

"To paraphrase your column, this all might be viewed as a relatively small flaw in the order of the universe if it did not happen so often."

This gentle-sounding man was saying he doesn't care to be treated like a freak when he enters a public place. He is a man with whom I can sympathize, and his letter made my day. From now on, whenever I am alone on public turf, I'm going to think of myself as a 6-foot, 7½-inch man.

The First Girl at Second Base

BETWEEN THE AGES OF SEVEN AND TEN, I spent a good deal of time dreaming of the day I would follow in the footsteps of my hero, Jacob Nelson (Nellie) Fox, and play second base for the Chicago White Sox. The crowd would roar as I stepped up to the plate in the bottom of the ninth with two out, runners on second and third, and the Sox trailing by one run. The roar would turn to whoops of joy as I, like the ever-reliable Nellie, punched a game-winning hit through the infield.

In endless conversations between innings at Comiskey Park, I badgered my grandfather about my desire to break the sex barrier in major league baseball. Nellie was small for a ballplayer—the sportscasters called him "Little Nell"—and it was quite possible that I might grow up to be as tall as he was. If Jackie Robinson (another of my heroes) could become the first Negro in the big leagues, there was no reason why Susan Jacoby could not become the first girl on the diamond. No reason at all, my grandfather agreed. He was too

softhearted to point out the facts of life to a granddaughter he had helped turn into a baseball nut.

Not all of my childhood heroes were sports figures,
but they all had one thing in common: They were men.
The most important nonsportsman in my pantheon was
Franklin D. Roosevelt, who captured my imagination
not because of anything he had done as President but
because he had overcome polio. I associated heroism
not only with courage but with the sort of courage that
is expressed in a visible, physical way. I had never
heard of any woman who embodied my notions of what
a hero did and was.

When I questioned my women friends about their
childhood heroes, an extraordinary number insisted
they never had any. Of those who did remember, all but
one acknowledged that their heroes had been men. It
turned out that the exception—a woman who said Margaret Sanger had been her hero—was speaking from a
newly acquired feminist consciousness rather than from
any true memory of childhood.

When I asked men the same question, nearly all of
them immediately produced long lists of heroes. All-
male lists. Not a single man grew up with a woman for
a hero. In fact, it seems that Eleanor Roosevelt was the
only public woman (apart from movie stars) whose
achievements impinged upon the consciousness of boys
who were growing up in the 1930's, 40's, and 50's.

Growing up in a culture with male criteria for heroism undoubtedly exerts its influence on a boy's image
of women. For a girl, though, the matter is more personal and more crucial: Her image of herself is at
stake. Hero worship confined to the opposite sex—a
phenomenon that seems to have been almost universal
among women of my generation and almost nonexistent
among men—poses a psychological problem on at least
two levels.

On the surface level—the rational one—the problem
is obvious and solvable. Reggie Jackson, who brought
on a bad relapse of my baseball hero worship by hitting
three home runs in the final game of this year's World
Series, is just my age. I was not at all surprised to read

in the sports pages that Jackie Robinson had been Reggie's hero as well as mine. The difference between us, of course, is that Reggie Jackson could grow up to play his hero's game.

The feminist movement has a sensible answer to the predicament of a girl who, having been born the wrong sex, can never grow up to be like her hero. Feminists say: "Give us our rightful place in the history books, establish equal opportunity for women now, and soon we'll have our share of heroes." Fair enough. A girl who dreams of achievement in sports or politics or law or medicine certainly has more women to emulate today than girls did when I was growing up.

The sensible feminist solution would be enough if a hero were only an object of emulation. The true function of the hero, however, lies in the realm of imagination. Most boys, after all, are no more likely to grow up to be Jackie Robinson than I was. Heroes give a child access to what the novelist Cynthia Ozick calls "the grand as if." When a young girl dreams of heroes, she dreams as if she were free: Limitations of height or weight or sex or race become irrelevant. A hero represents not so much a specific achievement as a whole range of human possibilities, an awe-inspiring glimpse of perfection.

On this level of awe and myth, it is difficult to develop a feminist alternative to the cultural values that have made both men and women regard heroism as a male characteristic. Heroism has almost always been linked with physical prowess and strength: Moral and physical courage are inseparable in most heroic sagas. This ideal of the hero places women at a disadvantage, because most societies have imposed severe restraints on public displays of female strength. Even today, when many of those restraints have crumbled, women are still at a disadvantage if the traditional concept of the hero is upheld. There is no getting around the fact that most men are stronger than most women.

Many adults talk about the need to smash traditional notions of heroism by stressing the moral rather than the physical aspects of courage. It sounds like a good idea, but I suspect these adults haven't been talking to many kids. In a sampling of my favorite ten-to-twelve-year-old girls, I elicited the name of just one woman hero: Billie Jean King. One of the girls expressed regret that her hero had trounced the aging Bobby Riggs rather than a man her own age. Two girls said their hero was the great Brazilian soccer player Pele, and two others, to my delight, mentioned Reggie Jackson. (I admit I spoke to the girls just a few days after the dramatic ending of the World Series.) One eleven-year-old said her ambition was to become a pilot and she was sorry America had never sent up a woman astronaut. So much for adult notions of dispensing with physical daring and achievement as standards of heroism.

There are people who think the end of the traditional hero would produce more realistic men and women. I doubt it. I still remember the pure joy I took in my baseball-playing fantasies. Doing well under extreme pressure was an important element in my fantasies, and that ideal is certainly suitable for any "realistic" adult. To dream as if you were free is a moving and beautiful experience—so beautiful that many adults feel obliged to forget it. I wish some of those dreams had come to me in the form of my own as well as of the opposite sex. Things ought to have changed by now, but it seems that barriers to women are more formidable in the world of heroes than in union hiring halls or executive suites.

—December 1977

Beyond the Ghetto

THE DAY after Carol Bellamy won the Democratic nomination for the New York City Council presidency, a man I know chuckled and said, "At last there's some competition for Bella." The same week, a woman editor asked me to do an article on how women hinder their chances for success by refusing to compete with members of their own sex. I turned down the assignment because I thought its premise was entirely mistaken.

It cannot be said often enough and loudly enough that the major obstacle to success for many women is not their alleged inability to compete with other women but their real inability to compete, in straightforward and unashamed fashion, with men. Women who think otherwise are kidding themselves. Men who imply otherwise are engaged in a not-so-subtle attempt to keep women in their place.

Consider the meaning of the "competition for Bella" remark. Apart from the fact that both are liberal Democrats, Carol Bellamy and Bella Abzug have almost nothing in common but their sex. They are of different political generations; they bear no resemblance to each other in their styles of campaigning or in their methods of getting things done in office. As the leading Democratic vote getter in the last election, Bellamy will certainly provide formidable future competition for almost anyone. The man who classified her with Abzug was really saying that the achievements of both women should be judged, not in a class with the accomplishments of other elected officials, but in a special subclass of lady politicians. He was also saying that there's no room for two prominent women in New York politics.

43

This gambit is as old as the secretarial pool. In a sleazy but embarrassingly insightful treatise called *The Girls in the Office* (the office is a thinly disguised Time Inc.), Jack Olsen reconstructed the reaction of a researcher who was turned down when she asked for a raise. "When I went to the manager for a merit raise, he was very pleasant but he put me off. He pointed at a lazy assistant who earned more than I did, and he said, 'As long as I have to pay her more than she's worth, I have to pay you less.' I had to agree with him. And I appreciated the implied compliment."

What a dummy, one thinks with the hindsight provided by fifteen years of the women's movement. How could she have failed to realize that her low salary was determined not by what other women researchers were making but by the fact that the system didn't allow women to move into the writing and editorial jobs reserved for men?

But the same gambit is now being applied to many of the well-paid, highly visible jobs that companies have opened up to women as a result of lawsuits and laws against sex discrimination. When I complimented a top executive of a news magazine about the promotion of a woman I know, he replied, "Yes, we had a lot of women competing for that job. She was far and away the best." Translation: "This job was reserved for a woman and she was the best one available. But don't think she could have beaten out a man for the job."

A ghetto job is a ghetto job as long as it is perceived by male executives—and by the woman they hire—as a job with a "for women only" sign. It doesn't matter whether the salary is $50,000 or $7,500 a year.

There is one important difference between the new ghetto jobs and the old ones: The new jobs can provide a real power base for a woman who is talented and realistic enough to take advantage of the opportunity. A sufficiently determined woman can use almost any responsible job to break out of the ghetto. One of the best examples of this process is offered by a woman I know—I'll call her Anne—who was appointed "vice president for consumer relations" of a large bank. Financial institutions frequently use consumer relations departments as dead ends for female executives—consumer relations being sufficiently removed from the real business of making and managing money.

Anne knew she was being offered a ghetto vice presidency, but she accepted the title because she wanted to use it as a lever to gain more responsibility. Within a year, she had convinced the bank president that there was a direct connection between the institution's poor consumer relations and its ailing personal loan program. She is now a vice president in charge of personal loans—a job with a much higher salary and real power. Two other women are handling her old consumer relations post, but neither of them has been given the title of vice president. Anne thinks her bosses are convinced that every woman will use the consumer relations department to take over a male executive's job.

A conscious decision to compete with men is essential to a woman's success in almost any job. It seems so obvious: Most good jobs, in blue-collar unions as well as in white-collar professions, are held by men. Most hiring is done by men. The situation can only be changed by women who regard themselves and are regarded by others as being plain excellent—not excellent only in comparison to other women.

The difficulty women have in asserting themselves around men shows itself in ways that are much more subtle—and much more pervasive—than reluctance to compete with a man for a specific job. For several years, I have been working on a book dealing with recent immigration to the United States. There are only a few specialists in the field, and I frequently find myself in the position of being the only woman panelist at seminars for government officials, scholars, and other journalists. Time and again, I have noticed that the women in the audience seldom speak up in the discussions following the formal speeches.

I particularly remember one seminar sponsored by the Smithsonian Institution, which had managed to corral nearly everyone who knows anything about immigration. At least a third of the audience participants were women. In the two-and-a-half-hour discussion that followed the panel, only one woman made a comment. When the evening ended, several woman came up to talk to me. I asked one why she hadn't added her comments to the general discussion and she said, "Oh, I just feel self-conscious in a roomful of people." What she meant, I am sure, is that she felt self-conscious in a roomful of men.

Work—outside the female ghetto—requires a delicate interplay of competition and cooperation with colleagues of both sexes. Most of the women I know do not have any trouble maintaining this delicate balance with other women. The problem arises with men, when the rules of the game can be changed by erotic tension as well as by sex discrimination.

Enough of the "competition for Bella" gambit. Rosalyn Yalow is a great scientist, not a competitor for the historical niche occupied by Marie Curie. Elizabeth I was a great queen, not just a rival of Mary Stuart's. Women who have "made it" are no longer pleased to be told that their achievements are remarkable—for a woman.

—February 1978

Kid Haters

"I WOULD LIKE to live my life in quiet, without being bothered by children, by churches, by schools," says a dashing young man with a mustache. An older man, who appears to be in his fifties, declares in bitter tones, "I moved to this community with the assurance that I would not be plagued with children."

These assorted sourpusses, who lend support to Shakespeare's contention that "crabbed age and youth cannot live together," put in an appearance on a recent broadcast of CBS-TV's "60 Minutes." They were tenants in the huge Marina del Rey apartment complex in Los Angeles, and they were complaining about the efforts of California parents to force landlords to rent to people with children. So far, the California courts have upheld the right of landlords to rent to "adults only."

The legal issues are fascinating. Marina del Rey, like every significant residential and recreational construction project during the last fifteen years, was built with a combination of direct and indirect subsidies from local and federal taxes. Nevertheless, more than 90 per cent of the apartments in the complex are off limits to taxpayers who happen to have children.

As "60 Minutes" pointed out, the problem is not restricted to Marina del Rey or to the state of California. Only four states have laws prohibiting landlords from refusing to rent to people with children. My own inspection of newspapers in a dozen large cities showed that between 50 and 75 per cent of the apartments listed in the want ads were for "adults only." If New York did not have a law prohibiting discrimination on the basis of parental status, it would take the landlords in this city about one week to up the ante for hard-pressed families.

The social values implicit in the comments of the tenants at Marina del Rey are even more fascinating—and a good deal more depressing—than the narrower legal issues raised by the suits against landlords. When I was growing up in the 1950's, mass-circulation magazines were constantly churning out articles that solemnly raised the question of whether America was becoming a totally child-oriented society. If this country ever was a child-centered society, the time for concern is long past. Americans retain an excessive reverence for "youth"—the relatively unlined faces, firm flesh, and awe-inspiring energy of the late teens and twenties—but there has been a dramatic shift in opinion about the value of having and raising children.

This change in values has been highly desirable insofar as it has freed people from the socially imposed compulsion to have children. Women in particular are benefiting from the abandonment of the idea that parenthood is everyone's sacred destiny. But the desirable emphasis on individual choice has produced a disturbing corollary, embodied in the comment of the young man who didn't want to be bothered by "children, schools, or churches." It is one thing to say "I don't want to have children." It is quite another to say "I don't want children and I don't give a damn about anyone else's kids either."

In an introduction to a study called *Two Worlds of Childhood: U.S. and U.S.S.R.*, Urie Bronfenbrenner, a social psychologist, asks, "How can we judge the worth of a society? On what basis can we predict how well a nation will survive and prosper? Many indices could be used for this purpose, among them the gross national product, the birth rate, crime statistics, mental health data, etc. In this book we pose yet another criterion: *the concern of one generation for the next.*"

The concern of one generation for the next is the fundamental compact binding every society—and it is a compact a growing number of Americans seem determined to ignore. The aggravation of apartment tenants who don't want tricycles cluttering up their halls is just one symptom of the erosion of this compact. School bond issues are being rejected in cities and suburbs throughout the country—not only because property taxes are high, but also because a great many people don't want to pay for the education of other people's children.

Activists in the women's movement, like other Americans, are divided on many issues involving children. This fact has been downplayed by feminist leaders, because they are worried about right-wing charges that the women's movement is out to destroy family life. Nevertheless, the split is a real one. I recently had a long argument with a well-known feminist writer who was denouncing the efforts of women who want to deduct the cost of child care from their income as a business expense. The same woman is opposed to public financing of day-care centers because, she says, "the government shouldn't be encouraging people to have more kids."

The most peculiar aspect of this attitude is that it treats children as a luxury. I resent paying taxes for Nelson Rockefeller's Albany Mall and for superhighways and, should it come to pass, for the maintenance of Radio City Music Hall. State officials with edifice complexes and gas-guzzling cars, and architectural monuments with shows the public won't pay to see, are, in my opinion, luxuries. Children are necessities. People who choose not to have their own children ought to be glad other people still want kids. I should point out that the Scrooge-like view of children is held by many people who have already raised families as well as by nonparents.

Even if one is impervious to the pleasures of associating with the younger generation, there are plenty of selfish economic reasons for concern over the fate of children. The sharp increases in Social Security taxes are already giving us a taste of what we can expect in a society with a growing proportion of older people who are unable to work. With fewer young people entering the labor force, those of us now in our thirties and forties and fifties can look forward to ever-increasing taxes to care for people who have retired. And, if the number of young workers continues to decline, who is going to keep the social security system solvent when we are in our sixties and seventies?

Of course, there is something terribly sad about having to make an economic argument for being interested in children. I honestly don't know why anyone wants to live in an "adults only" world. I do get annoyed when my next-door neighbor's daughter screams in the hall from 4 to 6 p.m., or when she leaves a crayon on the floor for me to trip over. But the annoyance is more than canceled out when she asks me some bright and charming question that makes me see how much she has grown in wisdom and age and grace during the past two years.

People who don't want to be "plagued" or "bothered" by children are really saying they don't want to be bothered by the creative and messy business known as life.

—February 1978

The kid haters turned out to be big letter writers. I have them to thank for an addition to my vocabulary: child free. That's right. As in "pest free," "roach free," "germ free." I wish the content of their letters was as funny as the style, but I just can't seem to laugh at these true believers. They scare the hell out of me. It's not that they want to maintain their "child-free life-style" in their own homes. (As you might expect, "life-style" is another of their favorite words; the jargon is as predictable as the lectures at an est session or the harangue of a Jehovah's Witness.) Like the people interviewed on "60 Minutes," they want the right to live in apartment complexes and whole communities that bar children— even though the communities may be developed with government loans and maintained through everyone's taxes. They don't want a cent of their own money spent for the services that children need. They want a child-free as well as a smoke-free environment in airplanes and restaurants. As a breed, they are completely unable to envision society as a cooperative effort between generations or between people of differing interests.

"It's people like you," wrote one woman, "who breed without regard to the needs of society, who want to destroy the rights of people who have made the mature choice of a child-free lifestyle. *My* money is supporting *your* children, but that isn't enough. No, you want to deny me any right to live without the howling and mess you have chosen to bring into the world. Visit a child-free home sometime. Or is it really ENVY that makes you so determined to take away my lifestyle?"

Most of my irate correspondents assumed I have children of my own. Just for the record, I don't. The one point on which these people and I agree is that we are lucky to be living at a time when women are not compelled to bear children and married couples are not compelled to raise families. But the child-free evangelists have a few compulsions of their own.

"If it is theft for the government to tax *you* in order to provide funds for highways—and believe me, it *is*—just where do you get off suggesting that it is O.K. for the government to steal *my* money to provide schools?

"Your attitude seems to be that while the 'good guys' like you, with your *so* obvious enthusiasm for the close company of children, are *worthy* of your rights, we child-free 'bad guys' are not—that we should not even be able to live in child-free areas if we so choose. That we are somehow *inferior* for preferring a serene landscape to one strewn with plastic tricycles and G.I. Joe dolls, and for valuing adult conversations over 'bright and charming questions'—usually the same one, repeated ad infinitum, I have found—that are your personal delight."

The child-free people are also big underliners of words. The following letter gets the prize for the most uses of "child-free" and "lifestyle" in one paragraph.

"As a couple with a child-free lifestyle, we are writing to tell you that politicians are finally going to have to pay attention to people who want to maintain a child-free lifestyle. The next generation, as you put it, is not the proper concern of those of us who have chosen a child-free lifestyle. We leave that to people who want the little darlings underfoot, who want to be taxed to death for schools and playgrounds, who want a lifestyle that deprives them of the ability to live in the present on behalf of the future. It is not those with a child-free lifestyle who should be taxed; those who do have children should pay a special tax every time they give birth, so that others do not have to bear the burdens they have inflicted on society."

The complimentary close was (I am not kidding), "Yours on behalf of the child-free lifestyle."

I suppose the term "child free" might be considered just retribution for the opprobrium that used to be attached to the word "childless" in the women's magazines of the 1950's. One can only hope that none of the child-free people ever faces the unfortunate set of circumstances that can produce an unplanned baby. Because you obviously can't teach your own baby to say "child free," so the little nipper's first word would, inevitably, be "lifestyle." And one thing the English-speaking world doesn't need is more people who go around talking about their lifestyles.

What Does a Woman Want?

"Candy and flowers, dear," Ellen had said time and again, "and perhaps a book of poetry or an album or a small bottle of Florida water are the only things a lady may accept from a gentleman. Never, never any expensive gift, even from your financé. And never any gifts of jewelry or wearing apparel, not even gloves or handkerchiefs. Should you accept such gifts, men would know you are no lady and would try to take liberties."

"Oh, dear," thought Scarlett, looking first at herself in the mirror and then at Rhett's unreadable face. "I simply can't tell him I won't accept it. It's too darling. I'd—I'd almost rather he took a liberty, if it was a very small one."

Such was Scarlett O'Hara's moral dilemma when Rhett Butler presented her with a green silk bonnet. I should be so lucky. The last gift I received from a man was not a silk frippery or a bottle of Florida water, whatever that is, but an eminently practical electronic calculator.

The calculator was certainly presented with the best of intentions. I had been complaining for weeks about what a drag it was to add up my business expenses and do my bank statements. I don't know what Scarlett's

mother would have said about calculators, but I do
know how I felt: I wanted to clobber the man who
brought me the infernal machine.

Even now, the calculator blinks at me reproachfully,
reminding me of its indispensability by its very proxim-
ity to my typewriter. Why do I resent this handy
gadget? Because, every time I look at it, I wonder what
it means when a man gives a woman a calculator instead of a fragile gold necklace or a dozen roses. Because there is no romance in its electronic innards. Because I can't stroke it or sniff it or wear it to bed.
Because, damn, damn, damn, it's just not the sort of
thing you expect a man to give a sex object. Poor calculator, symbol of the confusion that arises from a woman's dual desire to be admired for her gender-free mind
and to be lusted after (and not only in the heart) for
her female body.

It is impossible to overestimate the symbolic importance of gifts. When my mother sends me a beach dress
marked "Large"—ignoring the fact that I've only worn
"Smalls" since I shed my teen-age fat—I assume there's
a message buried in the tissue paper. When I send her a
pallid blue blouse with a bow at the neck—in a fussy
style she has not worn since the early 1950's—I assume
she finds a message too.

The tiffs inspired by gifts from members of the same
sex are insignificant in comparison to the emotional
storms triggered by gifts from members of the opposite
sex. Men who are wondering what to give their sweet-
hearts on Valentine's Day would do well to ponder the
symbolic message of their gifts on this hokey romantic
occasion. My father once made a terrible mistake by
presenting my mother with a new stainless-steel frying
pan. The fight that ensued remains a famous one, even
in a family much given to shouting and breaking crock-
ery in the heat of domestic battle. In all fairness, I must
admit that my mother's complaints about her old frying
pans were as loud as my recent complaints about having to do my own arithmetic. Nevertheless, I don't see
how my father could have thought Mother's complaints

meant she really wanted pots and pans for her birthday or wedding anniversary or Valentine's Day.

Men who want to arouse tender emotions rather than the ire of the women in their lives might begin with Jacoby's Law: The more intelligent and competent a woman is in her adult life, the less likely she is to have received an adequate amount of romantic attention in adolescence. If a girl was smart, and if she attended an American high school between 1930 and 1965, chances are that no one paid attention to anything but her brains unless she took the utmost care to conceal them.

Until I was fourteen, I attended parochial schools in which the nuns made a great effort to shield their charges from the brutal world of adolescent courtship. When we exchanged gifts at our eighth-grade Christmas party, Sister Cyril Therese made sure the unpopular kids would not be forgotten. Instead of giving presents to the people we liked best, everyone drew a name out of a hat. I was thrilled when the card on my package showed that it came from Bob Wheeler, who was generally thought to have the most sex appeal of any boy in the class. Bob didn't know I was alive; he was interested in the girls who knew how to tighten the belts of their green serge uniforms in a way that showed off their budding figures without attracting the wrath of the nuns.

It seemed to me that the happy accident of Bob's drawing my name for the Christmas party might form the basis for a whole new relationship. When I opened the box (carefully wrapped by his mother), I almost wept when I saw a sturdy pen-and-pencil set. Girls around me were opening little bottles of perfume and chains with artificial pearl drops. So much for the efforts of the nuns to shield us from the mysteries of sexual attraction.

Things didn't change in high school. When I was a junior, the movie *Breakfast at Tiffany's* was released; we all sighed when Audrey Hepburn's romantic fate was sealed with a ring from a Cracker Jack box. My best friend Wendy had an enterprising boyfriend who sent her flimsy ring off to Tiffany's with the request that it be polished and engraved. How we envied her when that ring came back in a velvet box. (Years later, a salesman at Tiffany's told me thousands of people had the same idea after the movie was released. The store decided it would be good public relations to polish all the rings at no charge. I can well believe that thousands of diamond rings were ultimately purchased at Tiffany's by the former Cracker Jack set.)

The year Wendy got her ring from Tiffany's, I did get a strange present I thought was intended as a romantic gesture. It was an eyelash curler. As it turned out, the boy who gave me the curler was picked up on charges of shoplifting at the local drugstore. Eyelash curlers, hanging loose on the Maybelline racks with eyebrow pencils and mascara, were irresistible bait for a kleptomaniac.

Which brings us to Valentine's Day. If a man is interested in a woman who was a cheerleader and was always invited to high school proms, he probably doesn't need to worry about the romantic portion of her ego. He can give her a tool kit or a calculator or a jack for tire changing and she will no doubt be thrilled that he appreciates her for something other than her looks. But if a woman was once sneered at for being a "brain," she would probably prefer the adult equivalent of a Cracker Jack ring. In return for such a gift, she might even allow a man a liberty—if it were a very small one.

—February 1978

Wardrobe Engineering

I HAVE LONG BLOND HAIR hanging well below my shoulders. I always carry a handbag, and have also been known to carry a briefcase when I am lugging around a stack of papers. My favorite colors are yellow, orange, and red; I don't own a single navy-blue suit.

I am marked for professional failure—or so say the men who are making a good deal of money writing books that tell women how to dress for success in business. I have seen the light and intend to mend my ways, but I feel an obligation to pass on some of this newly acquired sartorial wisdom to other women who may be doomed unless they are taken in hand by a "wardrobe engineer." Repent, Katharine Graham and Mary Wells Lawrence and Barbara Walters! Repent while there's still time.

John T. Molloy, who calls himself a "wardrobe engineer" (would I make up a job description like that?), sets forth two basic premises in *The Women's Dress for Success Book*. One is that women "cannot have equal status and equal pay without a collective image equal to that of men. Without a uniform there is no equality of image." The other is that "dressing to succeed in business and dressing to be sexually attractive are almost mutually exclusive." In Molloy's view, a sexually attractive image detracts from the business authority of both men and women.

Molloy takes himself very seriously and, lest you have any doubts, he informs you in the very first paragraph of his book that "wardrobe engineering" is based on that holy of holies, "scientific research."

56

What an ambitious woman should wear to work,
Molloy says, is a dark suit with a white or light-colored
blouse. He claims his research shows that women are
one-and-a-half times more likely to be treated as executives in a suit with a skirt than they are in any other
garment. (If a woman were four or five times more
likely to receive executive treatment, I might see some
justification for forcing us into such an uncomfortable
uniform. But why bother for such a slight edge?)

Molloy also reports enthusiastically on a "pledge" he
says was drafted by women in one corporation:

"I pledge to wear highly tailored, dark-colored traditionally designed skirted suits whenever possible to the
office, not to wear such outfits socially, and to encour-
age other women to do the same. I am doing this so
that women may have as effective a work uniform as
men and therefore be better able to compete on an
equal footing."

Something about this pledge sounded eerily familiar,
but it took me several days to dredge up the association
from the depths of my memory. At the parochial school
I attended, eighth-grade girls who were inducted into
the Sodality of Our Lady also had to take a pledge. We
promised to wear blouses buttoned up to our necks and
skirts long enough to touch the ground when we knelt;
we pledged to avoid all sweaters (unless they were
worn unbuttoned over a blouse).

The gist of Molloy's advice is that a woman who
hopes to succeed should adopt a look that resembles, if
not a nun's habit, the dreary garb required for men in
the 1950's. The irony, of course, is that men have acquired much more freedom in dress during the past fifteen years. Women, it seems, are now supposed to
adopt the undertaker image that a great many men
have abandoned.

Michael Korda is a good deal less authoritarian
about what women should wear in *Success! How Every
Man and Woman Can Achieve It*. The difference be-
tween the two men's advice may reflect the fact that
Korda works in the flamboyant offices of Simon &
Schuster while Molloy is a consultant to dun-colored

firms like Merrill Lynch, Pierce, Fenner & Smith. (I also suspect Korda of failing to take his own advice. Successful people, he has written, seldom appear "rumpled and sweaty." I swear on my copy of *Success!* that I have seen Michael Korda wheeling and dealing at literary cocktail parties where he looked both rumpled and sweaty. It wouldn't stop me from doing business with him, though. I sweat too.)

The contrast between Korda's and Molloy's advice gives one pause about listening to what any man has to say about what a successful woman should wear. Korda does mention the occasional usefulness of suits, but what he really likes is the Diane von Furstenberg wraparound dress. "It looks good on almost every figure, is acceptable under almost any social or business circumstance, is a recognizable status symbol, and is available almost anywhere in the country . . . If I were a woman in business, I'd buy a dozen of them."

I like Diane von Furstenberg dresses too. What Korda fails to mention is that their chief characteristic is they are sexy—not blatantly sexy, but agreeably draped to follow the lines of a woman's body. Which tells us only that Michael Korda likes sexy dresses and proves absolutely nothing about how a woman should dress for work.

In most of the "how to dress" books, there is a basic confusion between overt sex appeal—the special way a woman might dress when her lover is coming over for dinner—and the normal, everyday sexual attractiveness and attraction that are instrinsic to the image of any woman who takes pride in both her mind and her body. This sort of sex appeal is just as much a characteristic of proud and competent men as it is of proud and competent women.

Setting up a dichotomy between sexual attractiveness and professional competence places women in a no-win position. A woman can try to look as neuter and neutral as possible, but a body-concealing suit and an attaché case will not conceal the fact that she *is* a woman. If a woman feels most comfortable and attractive in a charcoal-gray suit, fine. But if she is putting on a "business uniform" because she wants to hide the liability of her sex, she is kowtowing to the primitive bias that maintains "a real woman" cannot be smart and successful.

These books also confuse clothing that projects overt sex appeal with clothing that is simply inappropriate for a business setting. I recently asked one of the most competent, sensitive executives I know to tell me what his reaction would be if a woman arrived for a job interview in a slinky, low-cut dress. Without a moment's hesitation, he said, "I'd think she was as crazy as a man who showed up for an interview in black tie and ruffled shirt."

It is insulting to suggest that any ambitious woman would show up for work in the costume of a go-go dancer. Molloy cautions women against wearing lace frills to the office; Korda warns against wearing T-shirts emblazoned with pornographic messages.

Aren't women lucky to have men who care enough to tell us not to wear pornographic T-shirts or peekaboo blouses? We never could have figured that out for ourselves.

—December 1977

Battering Back

A NEW FEMINIST HEROINE has arisen in the person of Francine Hughes, a thirty-year-old woman who put an end to her husband's brutal beatings by pouring gasoline around his bed and setting him aflame while he slept. A jury of ten women and two men in Lansing, Michigan, found Mrs. Hughes not guilty of murder by reason of temporary insanity.

What disturbs me is not the acquittal itself—who could want further punishment for a woman who had endured a man's punishing assaults for thirteen years?—but the fact that the case has become a feminist *cause célèbre*. Feminists who rallied to the support of Mrs. Hughes saw the issue as one of a woman's right to self-defense and the acquittal as a warning to millions of men who beat up their wives and children each year.

The brother of the slain man, interestingly, drew much the same conclusion from the jury's decision as the feminists did; the only difference was that he viewed the implications with dismay rather than enthusiasm. In a television interview he said, "I think this decision will give a lot of violent women an excuse to go out and commit violent acts . . . to take their revenge." I was watching the news with a friend who observed that "if revenge is what it takes for a woman to be in control of a situation like that, then I'm for it."

How, I asked my friend, can one possibly use the word "control" to describe the act of a woman so desperate, so driven, in such a state of psychic bondage that she could free herself from a brutal man only by killing him while he slept. It seems to me that the attitude of many feminists toward the Hughes case violates the basic feminist belief that women can and should take control of their own lives.

Those who maintain that Mrs. Hughes had a moral (as opposed to a legal) right to do what she did are suggesting that a woman who would not be victimized must turn murderous. As anyone who has studied the history of master-slave relations knows, the master's fear of violent retaliation has always coexisted with his assumption of the slave's passivity. But women are not slaves—or they do not have to be slaves.

Mrs. Hughes, like most women who endure long-term physical abuse from men, had assumed a number of psychological characteristics more commonly associated with slaves than with free human beings. The details of the case, most of which were omitted from national news accounts of the trial, are enlightening.

Newspaper articles generally referred to the dead

man as Mrs. Hughes's husband. He was, in fact, her former husband; she had divorced him in 1971 after seven years of marriage and four children. But it is perfectly reasonable to use the term "husband," because Mrs. Hughes continued to relate to him as a wife after the divorce. It was clear from her testimony that she remained bound to him emotionally, on many occasions sexually, and always as a victim and target for abuse.

But Mrs. Hughes did not play the role of the total victim. She was taking courses at a local business college because she wanted to support her children and get off welfare. On the day of his death, Mr. Hughes not only had beaten his wife several times but had forced her to burn her business-school textbooks in the back yard.

Francine Hughes was living in the same house with her former husband because she had agreed to nurse him back to health after a serious automobile accident. He had, of course, made a good enough recovery from his injuries to beat her up many times in gratitude for her care. This situation offers a classic and extreme example of the psychological victimization that characterizes battered wives. It is impossible to imagine a man returning with concern to the bedside of a wife who had systematically subjected him to physical torture.

The drama of the Hughes case arouses extraordinary interest in Lansing, which is my hometown. I discussed the case with several women friends there and found their reactions fell into two distinct categories. Some maintained that Francine Hughes was driven mad by years of humiliation and simply did not know what she was doing. Others said they were sure she *did* know what she was doing and that she "finally gave the creep what he deserved."

I do not think either of these reactions bodes well for the cause of women's rights. If we say Mrs. Hughes was crazy, we are equating self-assertion with insane violence. If we say she was sane and did the right thing, we are ruling out the rational means of self-defense that lie between victimization and murder.

There are other choices. A battered wife can leave

her husband. She can testify against him in court. She can become economically and emotionally self-sufficient and never go near the bum again. Or, in some cases, she can force the man to get the kind of help that might make it possible for him to change. (It does happen from time to time.)

These are not easy choices. Many areas of the country have no shelters to provide wives with temporary protection while they figure out how to cope with a brutal husband. Many policemen and law-enforcement agencies are unsympathetic. In a recent ABC-TV movie on battered wives, an indifferent policeman says, "A good punchin' around is what some of these women need to turn 'em on."

But the attitudes that have long enabled men to get away with wife beating are changing: The Hughes case is evidence of that. If a jury was willing to acquit a wife who set fire to a sleeping man, it would surely have listened with sympathy to the testimony of a woman who wanted to protect herself from the assaults of a living husband.

Battered wives today are in much the same situation as rape victims were ten years ago. The possibility for change exists, but it cannot become a reality unless women are willing to appear in court, to put their bruised bodies and minds on the line for essential changes in the law and in social services.

My reservations about the Hughes case are similar to the ones I held when Inez Garcia was tried in 1974 for the shooting of a man twenty minutes after an alleged rape. Mrs. Garcia's lawyer insisted at the trial that an "unwritten law" allows a woman "to take the law into her own hands to protect her integrity."

Unwritten laws used to allow men to kill their wives if they found them in bed with a lover. Unwritten laws required rape victims to defend their past sexual conduct. Unwritten laws intimidated wives into silence when their husbands beat them.

Feminists who advocate a woman's right to "self-defense" against a sleeping man—however brutal the man may have been—are really talking about the substitution of one unwritten law for another. What Francine Hughes and all of us need is a written law to protect us and the guts to use it.

—December 1977

Fear Taxes

SARA NEVER RIDES THE SUBWAY. She fears—not necessarily in the following order—murderers, rapists, purse snatchers, flashers, and all of the seamy types who take advantage of rush-hour crowds to rub up against women. Avoiding the subway costs Sara a good deal of time, because she lives at 91st and Madison and works at 41st and Lexington. It also costs her money, because she usually winds up taking a cab when her bus bogs down in midtown traffic.

I also know a great many men who dislike the subway, but they all manage to overcome their distaste in order to save time and money. Sara, however, is like many women: She feels herself to be utterly vulnerable on the city streets, and she "protects" herself by spending $40 to $50 a week on cabs. I once pointed out to her that she could afford to move out of her two-room apartment if she could only bring herself to take the subway. "I know," she said sadly, "but I'd be scared all the time."

This state of inner fear—shared by poor, rich, and middle-class women—is more debilitating to a woman's ego than any form of sex discrimination that comes from the outside. I am not talking about the awareness of crime that exists as a tick in the consciousness of most urban (and suburban) Americans, but about the belief of many women that they are vulnerable, not because they live on a badly lighted street, or work late at night, or lack concerned neighbors, but simply because they are women.

Overcoming this conviction of vulnerability is, I believe, central to the thought and action of a free woman.

It is no small matter to pay a "fear tax" of $40 a week to avoid the subway. Women who make less money than Sara—most of the working women in New York City—don't have the option of taking cabs once or twice a day. Some of them simply don't go out at night. Not ever.

Locking out the world after dark is particularly common among older women, who feel (with some justification) that the physical frailty of age makes them especially vulnerable. But I know a robust forty-year-old who behaves exactly the same way: When her husband goes away on business trips, she sighs and resigns herself to staying home in the evening.

There are endless variations on this theme. Women who won't go into Central Park—even in the daytime—because they really believe a rapist lurks behind every tree. Women who *never* talk to strange men—not at the intermission of a concert, or in a neighborhood restaurant, or sunning on the grass in a park. Women who won't take a walk in the evening when they get restless. Women who, in short, cannot experience the joy that accompanies a sense of personal liberty.

To break the hold of this fear, it is essential to separate the mythic aura of female vulnerability from the realistic caution that can reduce a woman's chances of becoming a crime victim.

There is no question that the sense of vulnerability shared by so many women is rooted in fear of rape—a fear that is usually instilled and reinforced by parents. Small children of both sexes are cautioned against taking candy from or getting into cars with strangers. For a boy, the parental admonitions usually end in adolescence, when it is presumed that he is physically able to take care of himself. For a girl, the admonitions are usually redoubled in adolescence, when it is presumed that she is still unable to take care of herself and is, in addition, especially vulnerable because of her budding sexuality.

These warnings to teen-age girls—and the feelings of vulnerability they engender—are not useful in adult life. Is an unarmed woman really in greater danger than an unarmed man if she is confronted with a knife or a gun (or the threat of a knife or gun)? Granted, women can be raped on occasions when men are only beaten up or murdered. Granted, women are at a slightly greater disadvantage because they are smaller and lighter than men. But neither of these facts is overwhelming enough to justify any woman's assumption that her sex marks her as a victim.

Women who shroud themselves in an aura of vulnerability are often reluctant to think about the practical steps that might keep them out of real danger. I was not one of those who snickered when feminist groups began organizing martial arts classes for women. Although I doubt that the judo acquired in such a course will really enable a 110-pound woman to defend herself against a 200-pound assailant (especially if he has a weapon), I do think the organizers were right to stress self-defense rather than passivity as the most effective response to the threat of crime.

To me, self-defense consists mainly of "street smarts" rather than of judo or karate. While walking on the long crosstown blocks on the Upper West Side, I have often been amazed to see lone women edging toward dark stoops and doorways. When a street is lined with dark stairwells and alleys, you are much better off walking by the curb or even in the roadway; no one can clamp a hand over your mouth and pull you off the sidewalk in one swift motion. And, should you have to scream, you are more likely to be heard from the center of the street than from an alley. Thinking about such matters is an active way to avoid confrontation through advance planning; failing to think about them can turn a woman into a passive victim in an instant.

I also believe in aggression (that's right, aggression—not the more polite "assertion") as the proper response to some of the more common assaults directed against women. I don't understand friends who say they won't ride the subway because they are "humiliated" by contact with flashers and "rubbers." I have only encountered two "rubbers" in my years of riding the subway; both times I raked their faces with my fingernails and yelled "Creep" in my loudest voice. It felt very, very good to see them flinch and slink off toward the exit doors.

My mother-in-law, who is in her seventies, is a woman I particularly admire because she has refused to succumb to the fear that paralyzes so many women her age. The street on which she lives has become so crowded with drug pushers during the past year that it's no longer safe or pleasant to walk east from Lexington Avenue. (Exactly why the city has allowed this to happen is a subject for another column.) My mother-in-law's response has not been to barricade herself in her apartment but to take the crosstown bus instead of walking. As she says, there's very little point in being alive if you're going to hide out and give criminals the freedom of the streets.

—January 1978

The Single Life: Rich and Poor, Male and Female

Last year I bought a town house and two dogs and moved in with a girl I really loved. It was the first time I'd made a solid commitment to anyone. She decided it wasn't what she wanted, so here I am by myself—a suburban homeowner with two toy poodles and no woman.

—A WASHINGTON DOCTOR

Swinging singles? They live somewhere else, not in this town. I've gone out on exactly three dates since my divorce a year and a half ago.
—A LANSING, MICHIGAN, SECRETARY

I'm my own woman and I like it just that way. I don't have to go down to a court and beg for child support my ex-husband won't pay anyhow. I drive my cab twelve hours a day, six days a week, and I bring home $150. I'm young, I'm tough, I do fine.
—AN ATLANTA TAXI DRIVER

The diversity of single life in the United States contradicts both the old-fashioned image of unmarried people as lonely losers and the current media-manufactured image of "swingles" who cavort through an endless round of bars, parties, and no-strings-attached sexual adventures. The adult single population, which jumped by two million a year during the sixties, is now approaching forty-nine million. The estimate includes men and women who have never been married, widows and widowers, the divorced and legally separated—everyone from new college graduates savoring their first taste of independence to retired people who live together instead of getting married because they want to collect two Social Security checks. In between, there are millions of single parents who cope with the problems and pleasures of both family and unmarried life.

Like any newly discovered minority, singles tend to be viewed by the majority in misleading, monolithic terms. Stereotypes about the unmarried frequently seem as ludicrous as the image of a black population with a universal sense of rhythm and love for watermelon. Single men and women in different areas of the country expressed a combination of dismay, resentment, and amusement when they were asked about their public image. "Five years ago I was used to hearing sorrowful comments about my 'loneliness,' " said a thirty-four-year-old executive with the Coca-Cola Company in Atlanta. "Now I get lecherous envy. From reading the press, you'd think that every girl is 36-24-36 and every guy lounges by a poolside and waits for the beautiful blondes to admire his rippling muscles. The truth just isn't very glamorous—some single people are happy and some aren't, just like married people."

None of the people I interviewed fitted into a neat newsmagazine-style picture of "the single life." Age, sex, location, and economic status are major factors contributing to the diversity and complexity of single life. Twenty-year-old singles have no more in common with forty-year-old singles than newly married people do with middle-aged couples. Single life in small towns differs radically from single life in large cities. In some respects, economic status has an even more significant impact on the lives of singles than of married couples. Married people often add one small income—usually the woman's—to a larger income—the man's—and use the combination to push into a higher stratum of society. Singles of both sexes must go it alone, and take a heavier tax bite into the bargain.

Not surprisingly, single life seems to satisfy the upper middle class more than any other group. Affluent singles need never choose between a tacky studio apartment and putting up with three roommates; they are spared the penny-pinching which takes some of the "swing" out of the lives of $90-a-week file clerks and gas-station attendants. Money is especially useful in combating loneliness, the No. 1 bogeyman of many singles. "The most satisfying single lives are dotted with unhappy love affairs and sexual droughts—times when you just don't meet anyone worth seeing," says a thirty-year-old Washington journalist. "If you have money, you can go to New York for a weekend or Europe for a month. It's not as easy to spend money to get yourself out of a rut when you're married. Maybe your mate isn't in the same mood you are and doesn't feel the need for a trip."

Without money, it is difficult to translate the theoretical freedoms afforded by the single life into reality. A thirty-six-year-old New York lawyer emphasized this point as he described his plans to close out a highly successful law practice because he wants to travel and try to write fiction. "Most of my friends think I'm crazy," he said, "but I've already made enough money to support myself comfortably for several years. I've spent most of my adult life accumulating money or looking after other people's money; now I'm going to use it to free myself. I've always wanted to write, and I plan to settle somewhere in Europe and see if I have any talent. If I don't, I can pick up the law practice again. If I were married, I doubt that I would be able to break away and do this 'crazy' thing. Some of my friends have children who are only a few years away from college. How could I throw over a career in that situation?

"It's important to me that I've been successful at something and that I do have money. My friends say to me, 'But what if you're an absolute failure at writing?' Well, what if I am? I won't starve, anyway, and I'm not a failure as a lawyer. It's very bourgeois and probably wrong, but I think most middle-class people fail to strike out in new directions because they are afraid of financial insecurity."

Small but growing numbers of upper-middle-class women are also enjoying the combination of money, success, and single freedom that was formerly a male preserve. Unlike college-educated men, these women frequently seem surprised by their monetary and professional success. "I've been surprised to find myself making such a good salary," said a twenty-nine-year-old Washington woman with a demanding legislative staff job on Capitol Hill. "Freedom and security and money and power are all bound together in our society. Rightly or wrongly, I always thought that someone else would provide those things for me, although I was determined to become 'someone' myself."

Even when they make substantial salaries, single women are less likely than men to make the kinds of financial investments which would assure their future economic security and independence. I talked with a group of eight Washington women in their late twenties and early thirties, most of them making between

$15,000 and $20,000 a year. Only two owned any stocks, and they attributed their investment to the relentless nagging of their parents. None owned houses or cooperative apartments. Several had jobs which offered an optional payroll-deduction pension plan, but none had taken the option. Their financial arrangements were typical of the single women I met throughout the country; most of the single men who were making $20,000 a year had investments to show for their salaries.

"Women aren't brought up to think about managing money alone," observed Ellen Sudo, who works for the Democratic Study Group in the House of Representatives. "Even when a single woman loves her work and knows she will always work regardless of marriage, there's a hangover from traditional upbringing. Until very recently, I've always thought of the single state as something impermanent. Now I feel that I want a home and I want it now—I don't want to wait for someone else to come along and make it for me. I have thought about buying a house, although I'm terrified of accumulating possessions. I've been renting a house for the last six months, and the landlord isn't sure he can let me have it next spring. I'd like to plant flower bulbs—it's a small thing but, damn it, I want to know whether I can have flowers next spring or not."

Upper-middle-class singles of both sexes talk constantly about choices—whether to travel or save money, buy houses or rent apartments, invest in stocks or pension plans, stay with the same company or change jobs. Such choices are as foreign to millions of blue-collar singles as they are to married people with six children. Most blue-collar workers do not hang out at Maxwell's Plum, and they do not live in expensive singles complexes with swimming pools, saunas, and night clubs. In every city, singles are acutely aware of class distinctions in places of entertainment and residence. Just as the older crowd moves on when teeny-boppers invade a bar, professionals tend to abandon a favored hangout when file clerks and bank tellers seem to be moving in. "These people are pushy," sniffed a young Atlanta engineer. "I've found two bars I really liked in the last year, and they were both taken over by swarms of girls looking for a 'college boy.' You want to be with your own kind of people."

Blue-collar singles look for their own kind of people in places like The Red Rail, a combination bar and dance hall on the outskirts of Lansing, Michigan—a city of 135,000, the state capital, and home of the Oldsmobile division of General Motors. With no cover charge, ninety-cent drinks, and a country-and-Western band, The Red Rail is jammed with file clerks and auto workers on weekend nights. There is no regional ambience; the bar might be in any American city large enough to support a modest amount of night life. The customers range in age from the early twenties through the mid-fifties. Some are married people pretending to be single, but most of the older patrons are divorced. Many of the middle-aged men arrive in bowling shirts imprinted with the numbers of their union locals; the young men arrive in everything from turtlenecks to immaculately pressed suits, white shirts, and ties. The women favor tight pants and tighter sweaters. Fifty-year-old men roam from table to table, trying not to wince when the younger women turn down their invitations to dance.

The band was winding down into a slow song as Peggy Ann Sears turned down an invitation from a middle-aged man whose greasy gray hair, wide bell-bottomed trousers, and flashing ruby ring suggested a combination of Liberace and Elvis Presley. He hung around the table and cracked several dirty jokes, following Red Rail etiquette, which dictates that a man cannot slink away too quickly lest everyone know he has been rejected as a dance partner.

"He's a well-known creep—that's spelled C-R-E-E-P," Peggy Ann said after her unwanted admirer had moved on to another table. She looked both older and younger than her twenty-nine years—older because she wore her hair in a page-boy-and-bangs style reminiscent of the fifties, younger because she was only five feet tall and constantly chewed a wad of gum between swallows of gin-and-tonic. "You've gotta turn down the creeps

on slow dances, unless you want to get squeezed and
worked over like a tomato in a supermarket. I come
here for one reason—because I love to dance—but
what man will believe that?

"I laugh when I read about how exciting the single
life is, what wonderful chances there are for a girl alone
today. 'That Cosmopolitan Girl!' Wow! I'm a secretary
to a man who owns a liquor store—the only other men
I meet are married liquor dealers. If it hadn't been for
my kids, I would've moved to a bigger town—maybe
Detroit—when my husband took off. But I bring home
$95 a week—before taxes, get that—and my mother
takes care of my two little girls while I'm working. With
my education, I wouldn't make much better money in a
big city but a hunk of my check would go for day care.
I just couldn't make it."

Before her divorce ten months ago, Peggy Ann was
taking night courses to qualify herself for a job as a
court reporter. She dropped the classes when her husband left her. "I really liked court reporting, and it pays
much better than what I'm doing now. But I had to go
to work full time, and I didn't see how I could be gone
every night too. It's too hard on the kids and my mom.
Maybe when they get to be school age I can make it out
of this dead-end job. Maybe."

Peggy Ann Sears illustrates a pervasive fact of life
for many single women—they simply do not make
enough money. The aggravating money shortages turn
to suffocating hardship for those with children. An esti-
mated 2,272,000 families fall into what the Census Bu-
reau defines as the "near-poor" category—those who
make between $4,274 and $5,345 a year. Of these families, nearly one third are headed by women. They are
the working poor, people who are usually too proud to
go on welfare but find it difficult to make enough
money for what the Department of Labor considers a
"moderate" standard of living. "I don't especially want
to get married again," Peggy Ann said in a defeated
tone. "But if I can manage to meet someone decent, I
probably will get married again for the sake of my kids.

They've never had a man around the house. And I don't want them to grow up with what I can give them on my salary. But in my job, it's just not easy to meet anyone."

Because most blue-collar and low-level white-collar workers are trapped in sex-segregated "job ghettos," blue-collar men and women find it difficult to meet potential partners. "There aren't any girls on the assembly line," said a twenty-five-year-old Oldsmobile worker. "I came here for work from a much smaller town, and I don't have any old girlfriends from high school. So there's really no place to meet girls except in a bar, preferably with dancing. I have this dream, see. Someday I'll go to a Michigan State football game and there will be a nice girl sitting next to me. We'll be able to talk to each other like normal people, because we're both just there to watch the game and not to pick someone up. Everything will be just natural, like when you were sitting in the same algebra class with girls in high school. And I won't have to go to bars any more. But I've been to lots of football games and the girls beside me always have a date."

I did meet some blue-collar singles who enjoyed their lives and their freedom. Patricia Grant, a thirty-two-year-old Atlanta cab driver, is the mother of eleven-and twelve-year-old boys. She is usually on the streets by 6:30 a.m. so she can make it home in time to spend the evening with her sons. "I work harder than a man to make do," she says. "This is still the South, and people will pass up a cab driven by a woman for one driven by a man. I agree with Shirley Chisholm—I get more static because I'm a woman than because I'm black. Hell, all the cab drivers in Atlanta are black. There are men who get into my cab and give me the business because I'm a woman—they think I'm just a whore trying to drum up clients. I set them straight, and they give me bigger tips because they're embarrassed."

Pat Grant has a "steady man," who also drives a cab, and she met him through her job. He works the same hours and manages to bring home $25 more a week than she does. "It's true," he says, "I see it with Pat—

it's just tougher for a woman alone. I'm not much of a swinger myself. My wife split and left me with three kids. Yeah, that's funny, it's the black man who's supposed to be irresponsible according to all those studies. People just ain't studies. A lot of Pat's and my friends ask us why we don't just get married and combine the kids. We think about it sometimes, but we're both a little scared of marriage. Pat sure doesn't want to be depending on anyone but herself again, and maybe I don't want to depend on a woman. But we help each other out a lot, the way married people do. Still, there's times when the kids are in bed and I open a beer—and I'm glad I'm alone." Pat is equally cautious about trying marriage a second time, and she takes considerable pride in the fact that she is making it alone. Out of her $150-a-week earnings, $10 goes into a savings account each Friday. "That's over $1,500 in the last three years," she says. "When my boys are old enough for college, the money is going to be there."

Socially, sexually, and economically, singles are usually better off in large cities like Atlanta than in small ones like Lansing. The sexual revolution has not bypassed towns the size of Lansing, but it still causes much more comment than it does in larger cities.

The middle-aged residents of an expensive apartment complex in East Lansing—a university town—were surprised one afternoon when a fellow tenant showed up at a poolside party with a woman he lived with and whom everyone assumed was his wife. When one of the neighbors introduced her as "Mrs. ——," the man cut in and said, "No way." He is a regional administrator for a well-known religious organization, and the incident was still a topic of conversation several months later.

The desire to escape gossip and social restrictions is an important factor in the migration of singles from small towns to medium-sized cities and from medium-sized cities to larger metropolitan areas. Some fast-growing cities like Atlanta and Dallas are special meccas for divorced people who found that small-town life began to pall when they were without a mate. Pat Grant moved from Macon to Atlanta six years ago primarily because "I couldn't have a boyfriend there without my mama knowing. She and my daddy were pillars of the Baptist Church. I couldn't have had any normal life as a woman without getting married again, even if the man took off the day after the ceremony. What you value most as a single person is people minding their own business, and you only get that in a big city."

Singles are at a particular social disadvantage in small cities with a limited number of cultural activities, restaurants, and public places of entertainment. Socializing goes on almost entirely in private homes and is controlled by married couples. The domination of social life by couples is irksome to older singles who have never been married, and especially to divorced people cut off from most of the friends they had when they were married. Beverly Cogbill, who works for the Georgia Labor Department, is another Atlanta refugee from Macon: "I kept running into my husband's friends all the time, and I was hardly ever included in anything, I sat there for four years, feeling sorry for myself. One Christmas I cried and cried. When I was through crying, I decided it was my last Christmas in Macon. So I moved here, got a much better job, and found a whole world of people like myself."

Social life is not the only area in which small-town prejudice surfaces against single people. A thirty-four-year-old Michigan State University faculty member found it was virtually impossible for a single man to rent a house in East Lansing. "People just have this image of a single man as an irresponsible person who has beer busts and will probably break up the joint," he says. "I've tried and tried to rent houses, and I always get turned down when they find out I'm not married. Lots of faculty members go away and rent their houses for the summer, but I've never been able to get into one."

This experience typifies the reverse side of the swinging single stereotype: Whatever their age, sex, economic status, or location, singles must contend with an image problem which frequently combines the old picture of the lonely loser with the new, excessively care-free stereotype. The special image of singles affects both their personal and professional lives.

A recent survey of fifty major corporations by the new national magazine *Single* found substantial evidence of discrimination against the unmarried. Although 80 per cent of the responding companies asserted that marriage was *not* essential to upward mobility, a majority indicated that only 2 per cent of their executives—including junior-management personnel—were single. More than 60 per cent of the respondents said that single executives tend to make snap judgments, and 25 per cent believed singles are generally "less stable" than their married counterparts.

Many single men in their mid-twenties confirmed this corporate attitude; they told me job interviewers always asked them why they were still unmarried. One personnel officer with an insurance company asked a twenty-seven-year-old Detroit man whether or not he "liked girls." An executive with another company said, "You don't look like an irresponsible sort of guy, but you've been living in the same place for four years and haven't found a wife. Why?" The young man replied that he had not yet found anyone with whom he wanted to spend the rest of his life. The executive chortled and said, "You still like a good fuck, that's it."

The single image does not work the same way for women in business. In general, executives seem to believe that marriage makes a man more reliable and a woman less reliable. Many middle-aged male bosses tend to assume that a woman will stay with a company forever if she has not married by her late twenties. They also assume that pregnancy will disrupt the careers of married women. When a thirty-six-year-old editor in a New York publishing house received a major promotion two years ago, her boss told her: "You're a real career girl. I know that I can count on you not to go get married and leave us." The executive was taken aback when the woman told him she had been married for three years.

The self-image of singles has improved substantially

as a result of the unprecedented growth in the single population during the past decade. "I've gotten a lot of headaches from my family because I'm not married," said a thirty-year-old Manhattan stockbroker. "A nice Jewish boy is supposed to get married as soon as he's out of college and started in business. I think there was always the unspoken thought lurking around: 'Could my baby boy be a homosexual?'

"Now, suddenly, I've become respectable again. All of the good little boys who got married are getting divorced. The other day my mother said to me, 'Well, Paul, at least you've still got a clean slate in life.' I can even take a girl home to meet my parents now. They're really great people, but I used to hate having them meet any woman I was dating because they'd start asking whether she was Reform, Conservative, or Orthodox— or maybe not Jewish at all—and how the wedding ceremony could be performed if there were religious complications."

Jerry Zweig, a forty-three-year-old floor-covering distributor from Jersey City, New Jersey, remembers that "for the first year after my divorce, I was even embarrassed to say the word. I felt it was like talking about a terrible disease. Now there are so many people like me that I don't feel ashamed. I'm not opposed to marriage. I'd like to get married again, but I want to take time to learn some things about myself. I see this as a perfectly legitimate desire now. When I was in my twenties and early thirties, the idea would have been unthinkable."

It is probably too early to tell whether the sharp rise in the single population indicates a radically new way of life or simply a shift in the timing of marriages. Most of the singles I interviewed, including both the divorced and the never married, expressed opposition to early and hasty marriages rather than to the idea of marriage itself.

The millions of young singles who are taking more time to choose their mates could contribute to greater marital stability in the nineteen-eighties and nineties (although this is only a hypothesis based on past marital patterns). Many men and women who had emerged from bitter divorces said they felt their marriages would never have failed if they had "grown up" as singles before they took on the responsibility of a family. "If I were just getting out of college today," said one woman, "I wouldn't be getting married right away. Fifteen years ago, I felt like a freak because I was twenty-one and unmarried. Now I have to do the growing up I should have done then, and I won't get married again until I feel I am fully mature. But I'm not afraid of trying a second marriage when I do reach that point of maturity."

It is certainly a mistake to assume that unattached men and women in their twenties will remain permanently in the singles fold. Managers of singles apartment complexes say they have a high tenant turnover primarily because so many residents leave them to get married.

Although there were exceptions, single men and women generally felt their attitudes toward marriage had become more positive as they had grown older. Never-married singles in their late twenties and early thirties usually expressed a deep interest in forming long-term relationships. "I don't necessarily want to marry," says thirty-year-old Joel Pickelner, "but I'm certainly not ideologically opposed to the idea of marriage. I would like to settle down. I've had my fill of a nomadic sort of life. If I met a girl I loved and she wanted to get married, I think I'd be glad to. If she didn't want to get married but just to live together, that would probably be all right too."

Members of both sexes frequently mentioned children as a reason for shifting from singlehood to marriage. "I think about kids all the time," said a thirty-two-year-old man. "When I meet a new woman, there's always the question in the back of my mind: 'Could we be good enough together to be responsible for a new individual?' " Many singles echoed the views of twenty-nine-year-old Evelyn Wolfson, a Brooklyn teacher:

"If you'd asked me about being single four years ago,

I would have said it was the greatest thing in the world. I still think it's great for a lot of people, especially in contrast to immature marriages. But, quite frankly, I want to get married now. I want children, and I'm middle class enough to think I'd never have one while I wasn't married. Also, I love my work and I don't see how you could manage a child and a job without a mate to help you. I can be alone, often I want to be alone, but I don't want to stay alone for the rest of my life. I'm not desperate to get married, but marriage is the big, tantalizing unanswered question in my life."

The Great Couple-Friendship Fiction

A RUSSIAN FRIEND, an émigré writer who recently arrived in the United States, was telling me of his astonishment at the peculiar American institution of couple friendship. "When Americans are married," he observed, "you are expected to be friends with both or with neither. You pretend you want to see the two of them when you only want to see one; they pretend they both want to see you when one of them goes to sleep at the very sound of your voice. It's all very strange to me."

It is strange—or it would seem so in almost any other society or any other period of history. The Great Couple-Friendship Fiction, maintained by people who live together as well as by the married, ranks right up there with the lies women and men tell each other about sex and money in an effort to continue their lives together with a minimum of painful confrontation.

I suspect that couple friendship, like so many American institutions gone awry, originated in the best of intentions—the desire of middle-class Americans to free themselves from the rigid separation of the sexes that has marked the social life of both the rich and the poor throughout much of history.

Many of us are the grandchildren of immigrants who came from towns where men went off to cafés and taverns at night while women congregated in their homes. Better the compulsory coupledom of back-yard barbecues and balanced dinner parties—or so we thought. The trouble is that the social life of post-World War II America has made it almost impossible for anyone who makes up one half of a pair to sustain a serious individual friendship with an outsider of either sex.

"Two may talk and one may hear," Emerson wrote in an essay on friendship, "but three cannot take part in a conversation of the most sincere and searching sort." Not to mention four or six or eight. Most of us know Emerson was right, but we cannot reconcile the knowledge with the expectation that friendships should be incorporated into our marriages.

So we substitute "an active social life"—cocktail parties, dinners, brunches, weekends in the country filled with tennis and more cocktail and dinner parties—for the deeper enjoyment of true friendship. We talk wistfully about how hard it is to make a friend when you are over thirty; our talk is tinged with the same nostalgia that marks reminiscences of what it was like to make love in broad daylight on the living-room rug before the children came.

If we want a friend to ourselves, it is an admission that the person who shares our life cannot satisfy all our needs. This admission is somewhat less frightening when it involves a friend of the same sex than one of the opposite sex, but I am convinced that the added element of sexual jealousy evokes a response that differs only in degree. All close friendships that exclude a mate pose a threat to conventional notions of couple solidarity.

"It's like a slap in the face to me if my wife chooses to go out for the evening with a girl—oops, woman—friend instead of me," says a man I know who is both possessive and unusually candid. "It's as if she is saying, 'I'll enjoy what I'm doing tonight more with someone else than with you.' "

Exactly.

Two summers ago, I went to the theater with a close woman friend to see Julie Harris play Emily Dickinson in *The Belle of Amherst*. I particularly wanted to share the experience with my friend because she is a woman whose original mind and literary sensibilities invariably enrich my own perceptions. I didn't want to see the play with her husband. I didn't want to see it with *my* husband. The occasion stands out in my mind not only because it was a wonderful blend of art and conversation but because my friend and I haven't managed since to spend an evening alone together without the men.

The after-dinner hours, like weekends, are sacred marital turf. Each partner may be immersed in his or her own work, dreams, or football game on TV, but all's right with the couple world as long as both people are spending the evening under the same roof.

The couple-friendship fiction is upheld with even greater determination when a mate has a close friend of the opposite sex. One of my oldest friends is a newspaper reporter married to a woman who is a tax lawyer. She has always disliked his newspaper friends in general and me in particular. My friend and I see each other a maximum of two or three times a year when one of us makes it to the other's town on a business trip. To avoid a fight, he lies to his wife when we go out for lunch or dinner. The situation bothers me, but it doesn't bother me enough to end a twelve-year friendship or—almost as bad—to sit through dreary three-way meals in which the pleasure of two friends is destroyed by the boredom and antipathy of a third person.

It seems to me that women have the biggest stake in ending the fiction of couple friendship, which so often shows itself as a heartrending fraud when a marriage breaks up. Although conventional wisdom would have us believe that most social arrangements are made by women, the reality is that much of what passes for social life flows from the job held by the more powerful member of the couple. Society and sex discrimination still being what they are, the most important job is usually held by the man. I am thinking of one friend who was recently divorced from a well-known history professor. She got their house in East Hampton, but there is no one to fill it. Nearly all of their "friends" were among the "perks" of his position. They don't drop by to see her.

Even if a woman is lucky enough to remain happily mated, she will almost certainly spend the last ten to fifteen years of her life as a widow. The gap in life expectancy between men and women shows itself in this sad statistic: Of all living Americans over the age of sixty-five, more than 70 per cent of the men but only 30 per cent of the women are married. I don't know if it is possible to restore and expand the capacity for genuine friendship if it has been confined to one person for most of a lifetime.

I do know that I would like to go to the theater with women friends more than once a year. And I would like to have lunch with my old newspaper colleague without being made a conspirator in a silly and unnecessary deception.

—December 1977

This column prompted dozens of letters from men and women ranging in age from twenty-two to seventy-nine. All were, or had been, married and all said they regarded maintaining independent friendships as a serious marital problem. Some had worked out the problem within their marriages and some had not.

"This is not a problem that can be solved in a day or a year," wrote a seventy-eight-year-old widower from California. "When my wife and I were married in 1931, I played a jazz piano in night clubs for fun. She always resented it, because I would be away from home two nights a week, and she didn't want to come along with me because she was a teetotaler and didn't approve of the atmosphere. We fought about it for years—I never gave up the piano entirely, but she never gave up nagging me about it.

"Then our youngest child left home, and my wife decided she wanted to go to college. (You will realize, please, that this was before 'women's lib' and it wasn't all that usual for a grown woman to go back to school.) Well, I didn't really see why she wanted to do it, and I said so. She said, 'You've had your damn piano playing all these years, and I want something of my own.' That made a certain amount of sense to me. My wife eventually got her doctorate in art history and became the curator of a small local museum. I never knew very much about art, and she wasn't all that crazy about my friends in the music world, but after thirty-years of marriage, we had grown big enough to allow each other independent interests without being jealous. I should tell you that we shared everything else, but I truly believe we were larger people for allowing each other to grow. But how we used to fight about this. Married people, however much they love each other, are *not* Siamese twins."

The most poignant letter about the dangers of depending exclusively on one's mate came from a fifty-year-old widow in Brooklyn.

Dear Miss Jacoby,

I read your column with tears in my eyes, and I wanted to write and tell you how right you are. I was married for twenty-eight years, and my husband died nine months ago of a sudden heart attack. I know this sounds old-fashioned, but it always seemed to me that we had a perfect marriage. He was my lover and my intellectual companion and my best friend; I never felt the need for anyone else, man or woman.

I used to make fun of the women in my neighborhood for going to concerts or Wednesday matinees with each other. Their husbands weren't interested in those things, but my husband and I shared a love of music and the theater. In all our years of marriage, we were only apart for three nights—when I went home to stay with my mother after my father died. I was proud of that, proud of our devotion, proud that we would always rather be with each other than with anyone else. Sam always used to say, "Why should I stop off for a drink at a bar when I can come home to you?"

It was beautiful, but it ended when my husband died. I have no one. Our one daughter is living her own life in California, and I only see her twice a year. Anyway, you can't depend on a grown child to make your life full. The women in the neighborhood are kind, but I don't really belong to their groups. I never felt the need to make friends while my husband was alive, and now I am terrified that I have forgotten how to do so. I haven't met a new person by myself in years; I don't know what to say.

In all truth, I must say that I had been lonely for some years before my husband died, ever since our daughter went away. I was his best friend too, but he also had his acquaintances at work. I was beginning to think that I should look for a job, even a very menial job, just as a way of being with other people. Now, I am fortunate because my husband left me financially well fixed, but I am thinking of looking for a job again as a way of making friends. You are right: Women should realize that part of their lives will be spent alone and that they should keep a life of their own, even in a good marriage. I wonder if it is too late for me to begin?

Such Good Friends
(Masculine Gender)

IT IS A MAY AFTERNOON, and I am sun-bathing in the park near my apartment building with a man who has been my friend and upstairs neighbor for two years. On this bright and beautiful day, Josh is in a state of acute anxiety because his ex-wife is about to leave for a three-month vacation and his ten-year-old son is coming to live with him for the entire summer.

"I'm very excited about it," he says, "because it's the first chance I've had to be a full-time father since the divorce. But I'm also scared about whether I'm going to make the grade. I mean, Daddy is great when you come into the city on weekends and he takes you to the movies or a ball game, but my kid has never seen the daddy who comes home from work in a foul mood."

In the middle of the conversation, Josh's friend David—who is also his colleague at the university where they both teach—lopes across the grass toward us. The personal talk comes to an abrupt end. "Hey, Dave," says my friend, the worried father, "did you hear the departmental budget has been cut back by $25,000?"

Josh told me later that he considered David one of his closest male friends. Why, I asked, had he changed the subject from his anxiety about being a good father to the university budget. "Oh, you know," he replied, "it's so much easier to talk about personal stuff to a woman."

This incident speaks volumes about the limitations American men place upon their friendships with other men—and about the extra burden they place upon their relationships with women. Public activity, not private emotion, forms the core of most male friendships. Women—as wives, lovers, co-workers, or "just friends" —supply the emotional intimacy that men do not permit themselves to experience with one another.

The role of women as the sole outlet for men's emotions is a phenomenon that complicates relations between the sexes on many levels. At work, women often become the recipients of intimate confidences from male colleagues with whom they previously shared nothing more intimate than a take-out sandwich. At home, a wife may be overwhelmed by the realization that she is no longer in the enviable position of being "a woman, a lover, a friend" but in the near-impossible position of being her husband's *only* close friend. In situations where she draws some of her emotional sustenance from other women, he has only her.

It is impossible to consider the nature of male friendship—the ways in which it differs from female friendship, its importance in men's lives, its impact on relations between men and women—without establishing exactly what is meant by a "friend."

In a pioneering study of adult development called *The Seasons of a Man's Life,* psychologist Daniel J. Levinson observed that the distinction between a friend and an acquaintance is often blurred by men. "A man may have a wide social network in which he has amicable, 'friendly' relationships with many men and perhaps a few women," Levinson noted. "In general, however, men do not have an intimate male friend of the kind they recall fondly from boyhood or youth . . . We need to understand why friendship is so rare, and what consequences this deprivation has for adult life."

"Intimate" is the key word. Playing golf together or working together or watching a football game together does not mean that two people are friends, though friends may do any or all of these things with each other. In his essay on friendship, Emerson defined a friend as "a person with whom I may be sincere. Before him, I may think aloud." It is this high standard, with its implicit components of intimacy and trust, that I use when I speak of friendship. And, I would add, sincerity involves the sharing of emotion as well as thought. My upstairs neighbor and his university colleague are not really friends—they are friendly acquaintances in the same profession.

There are, of course, some men who have trusting and intimate friendships with other men, just as there are women who have only the most distant and circumscribed friendships with other women. Nevertheless, the traditional (and still widely accepted) standards of masculinity in American society do work against intimacy between men, while standards of femininity tend to promote intimacy between women.

These standards divide the world into the "masculine" realm of activity and the "feminine" realm of feeling. There have always been men who realized this dichotomy was nonsensical, and the women's movement has fostered a more widespread skepticism toward traditional assumptions about masculinity and femininity. In their heads, a great many men know that neither sex has a monopoly on activity or feeling. In their guts, they still feel the old split between "masculine" activity and "feminine" emotion. This split leads some men to screen their personal lives from other men in a way that women would find truly bizarre.

A thirty-five-year-old lawyer gave me a dramatic example of the reluctance of certain men to share personal feelings—and personal information—with other men. He overheard a conversation in the locker room of his athletic club between two partners in his law firm. They were discussing the startling news that a third partner—a man they had known twenty years—had a hemophiliac son.

"How did you find out about it?" one man asked the other.

"My wife saw a sign at our local high school that the Red Cross was having a blood drive for this kid. So I gave a pint of blood and I guess they got a list of donors, because Jack came over at lunch to thank me. I didn't know what to say, so I didn't say anything. Makes me feel like hell. God, what a burden to carry around. He never said a word all these years. I suppose it would be even worse if you went around crying on other people's shoulders about something like that."

These men were all in their mid-forties and had all been associated with the same firm since graduating from law school. I find it impossible to imagine three women whose lives had been connected for that length of time—whether through an office or a PTA group— who would have failed to share a personal problem of such magnitude.

The belief, usually instilled in childhood, that displays of emotion are "unmanly" is a powerful factor limiting the friendships of adult men. Some men say they worry about what they consider the ultimate femi-

nine breakdown—tears—if they reveal their emotions
before another man.

One man I know, who describes himself as "a real
crybaby since I was a kid," says he has always managed—sometimes with considerable effort—to avoid
crying in the presence of other men. "I've cried in front
of just one member of my own sex," he says, "and
that's my five-year-old son. I would never have cried in
front of my own father, even when I was little, because
I wanted to 'be a man' for him. I suppose allowing my
son to see me lose control is part of a conscious decision that I don't want him to think a man is someone
who never cries."

The cultural prohibition against physical displays of
emotion—whether in the form of tears or embraces—is
not a trivial matter. (Some participants in the so-called
men's movement have, inevitably, managed to trivialize
the issue by organizing "consciousness-raising" sessions
in which men are supposed to practice crying in front of
one another. The notion of a group of men learning to
cry on command induces giggles rather than tears.)

The development of genuine emotional intimacy between American men is unquestionably inhibited by
men's fears that displays of physical affection are in
some way tinged with homosexuality. How, for instance, can one cry in the presence of a person one is
forbidden to touch? No one would assume that two
women were lesbians because one was crying and the
other was comforting her in an embrace, but the same
gesture between two unrelated heterosexual men is almost unimaginable in our culture. Even between fathers
and their adult sons, embraces are usually restricted to
moments of great family stress.

The taboo against physical affection influences men's
behavior in both mundane and extraordinary situations.
One of my friends, a bachelor who loves to cook and
entertain women in his apartment, is reluctant to issue
similar invitations to men. When he sees men, he
usually meets them in a restaurant or bar. "I feel funny
saying, 'Come on over and I'll cook dinner for you,' to
a man. I didn't really think about it until I dropped by

a woman's house for a drink before dinner. She was expecting another woman, and she had set the table with nice china and flowers. I remember thinking it would seem just a little bit funny if I set a table like that for another man. And then, I envied her that kind of freedom. I feel free to present my domestic self—which is certainly part of friendship—to a woman, but not to a man."

Mark Stein, a forty-year-old teacher, told me how one of his colleagues at work had helped him through a lengthy personal crisis. His forty-one-year-old wife was confined to a hospital bed for three months in an effort to carry a much-wanted child to full term. His colleague, who lived in a nearby apartment building, happened to see Mark coming out of the hospital one night. After hearing the story, he began to make a habit of meeting Mark for a drink or a sandwich after visiting hours. He and his wife were in the waiting room on the night the Steins' baby was successfully delivered by Caesarean section.

"When they told me my wife and baby were O.K.," Mark recalls, "I broke down and started to cry. I put my arms around my friend's wife—I'd never met her before—and put my head in her lap. It was her husband who had seen the thing through with me, and he kind of turned his back. She was a woman, and even though I didn't know her, I could cry in front of her. If she hadn't been there, I suppose I would have bottled it all up."

Sporadic releases of emotion do not necessarily attest to the presence of true friendship but they are, for most people, essential to the development of a deeper, sustained intimacy. Mark Stein has not seen his colleague outside of work since his baby was born. "It was like a door closing," he says. "My wife can't understand it, because I told her what a help John was to me while she was in the hospital. I don't fully understand it myself. But I felt some kind of a breach that last night, and I think he felt it too. I don't know if it was because he saw me at my weakest, with my head in a woman's lap, or if it was because I should have thrown my arms around him instead. *He* was the person who had be-friended me. *She* was someone I didn't know. It's all very complicated."

It is all very complicated—for men and for women, who are expected to meet the emotional needs that are excluded from the ordinary canons of male friendship. I once discussed this subject with Joseph Brodsky, a re-nowned Russian poet who emigrated from the Soviet Union in 1972. In Russian society, intimate friendships between men are the rule rather than the exception. "One thing that was very striking to me when I came to America," Brodsky said, "was the great demand that a man here makes on his 'special woman.' Only with the special woman can he afford to be human. But if you can only be human with one person, how human are you? And how can a woman bear the pressure of being the sole object of her husband's humanity?"

The feeling that one is expected to be all things to a man places a heavy burden on any love relationship; that burden is never greater than in marriage, when the demands of day-to-day intimacy can turn claustropho-bic if one or both partners lack individual friends.

A woman married to a man who spends most of his free time in proverbial outings with the boys might wel-come a husband who devoted more time to emotional contact with his wife. But many women—a far greater number than one would believe from the endless psycho-babble about the need for more "communica-tion"—are simply overwhelmed by the realization that they are the only outlet for a man's emotions.

The pressure becomes most acute when people en-counter the inevitable problems that cry out for discus-sion with someone outside the intimacy of the couple. When a woman has a problem she feels she cannot talk over with her man—whether it concerns him or not—she usually turns to another woman. When a man has a problem he feels he cannot talk over with his "special woman," he, too, turns to another woman. She may not be "the other woman" in a sexual sense but, simply, the nearest female listener. One man told me, with consid-erable embarrassment, about the way in which he imposed a serious personal problem on a woman co-worker.

"About ten years ago, I was impotent for six months while my wife and I were going through a terrible period in our marriage. Remember, that was before there were magazine articles all over the place talking about things like that. I was simply terrified.

"I made an appointment with a psychiatrist—a man—and I broke it. Then one night after work I found myself pouring out the story to a woman colleague. I don't mean in a bar or over dinner, but when we're walking out of the office. I was really ashamed of myself—I'm sure the last thing she wanted to hear was something so personal from someone she worked with. We were friends, but not that close.

"The point is that she was very kind, very helpful—I must have picked her because she seemed like a sympathetic person. She told me she had known other men who had been through the same thing. Eureka! It was like one of those bulbs that light up over the heads of characters in comic strips. That sounds pretty naïve in 1978, I know, but in 1967 I really believed I was the only man in the world who had ever been through this experience. Embarrassed as I was talking to a woman, it would have been worse with a man. Yeah, it would have been admitting that *I* wasn't as much of a man as *he* was."

The tendency of men to seek out women colleagues as personal confidantes can prove to be a minor irritant or a major problem for working women. Like office affairs, close personal friendships can sometimes complicate relations on the job, especially if the man doing the confiding is either a woman's boss or her subordinate.

Some women bosses, feeling they cannot (and perhaps do not want to) avoid the personal confidences of men, turn the situation to their advantage by making "mothering" a part of their executive style. Women who are subordinate to or on an equal footing with their male colleagues sometimes adopt the posture of a friendly "sister," while maintaining a taboo against office sex. (The woman worker as friend and surrogate sister is an image that appeals to a great many women as well as to men. The durable popularity of "The Mary Tyler Moore Show," for example, was based on just such a role. Remember Good Old Mary, helping Murray and Ted and Lou solve all of their problems? Mary even showed the men how to become better friends with one another. Would Lou have agonized over the possibility that Ted might be sterile? Would Murray have helped Lou through the trauma of selling his house after a divorce?)

In sexual (or potentially sexual) relationships with women, a man's unmet needs for nonsexual intimacy can contribute to a confusing and ambiguous mix of emotions. When a man makes a friendly overture to a woman, she automatically registers the possibility that they might become more than "just friends." But when a man makes an outright sexual advance—or when he says he has fallen in love—a woman seldom acknowledges the possibility that what he really wants may be "just a friend."

Years ago, I lay in bed with a man I loved and listened to him talk about the bitter breakup of his marriage. "I've never been able to talk about it before," Philip told me. "It's like a stone melting inside me."

"You can't mean you never told Dan about any of this," I replied. Dan, a novelist, was Philip's oldest adult friend: They had known each other in college, lived in the same city, and saw each other several times a month.

"Oh sure, Dan knew I was miserable," Philip said, "but I didn't talk about any of the details." Then, only half-jokingly, "I didn't want to wind up as one of the characters in his books."

I had two distinct reactions—shock that Philip did not really trust the man he considered his best friend and the nervous sensation that I was probably the wrong person to hear the story of his marital breakup for the first time. I had only known Philip a few months, and I could not help but feel that an old friend might have provided more genuine understanding and effective support than a new lover.

Much later, I had a third realization—that I was not loved. Philip needed someone to talk to. He needed a woman, because he couldn't bring himself to talk to a man. So he "fell in love." In the same situation, I would have picked up the phone and called one of the women who are my closest friends.

There are signs that some men are beginning to reexamine the attitudes that have inhibited the development of male friendship in the past. The women's movement, with its attack on the old stereotypes of masculinity and femininity, has played a role in this re-evaluation.

Many men I know have developed a new respect for the role talk plays in cementing female friendships—the same talk that used to be ridiculed in jokes about the suburban *Kaffeklatsch* or the "feminine" habit of tying up the telephone for hours. In the past, many activity-centered male friendships have been conducted without the sort of conversation that is essential to intimacy.

Every friendship, of course, begins with activity—whether the activity involves school, work, or taking children to a playground. But school ends, people change jobs, and children grow up; unless a solid emotional foundation has been laid, the "friendship" ends when the activity ends. The lack of such an emotional foundation contributes to the "friendship vacuum" that Daniel Levinson observed in his study: Ostensibly close relationships, developed within highly structured situations like wartime combat, tend to disintegrate as soon as the shared activity is over.

More men are beginning to face up to the real pain and deprivation that can accompany an inability to acknowledge emotional connections with other men. *New York Times* columnist John Leonard conveyed this feeling in an article that was really a personal obituary for a friend and colleague who died of a heart attack on a tennis court. The column described the man's personal attributes and concluded, "I never told him I loved him."

Acknowledging the need for emotional support from other men does not make it easy to change the social patterns of a lifetime. My friend Josh—the one whose son is living with him for the first time since his divorce—took the first step when the boy attacked him bitterly for having "walked out" on him and his mother.

"I didn't know what to say. My ex-wife and I had agreed that our kid had taken the divorce very well, that he didn't seem to have any problems. My first impulse was to call her. Then I thought about calling my girlfriend. Then I thought no, this is crazy, I have a good friend at work, a guy who has three kids and was divorced three years ago. So I took him out to lunch—feeling funny about bringing up personal things. Not only was he helpful, but he was glad to have someone to talk to himself."

Then Josh gave me as succinct an explanation as I have ever heard of why strengthened male friendships are good for women as well as men.

"For the first time, you know, I wasn't dumping a problem on a woman—my ex-wife or anyone else—that was really my problem."

—*October 1978*

The Price of Pregnancy: Who Pays?

DAN WAKEFIELD, the novelist who developed the idea for a new television series called "James at 15," resigned from the show because the network would not tolerate a euphemistic reference to birth control in an episode depicting the young hero's loss of his virginity. Wakefield wanted the boy to ask the girl if she was "responsible" before intercourse. This formulation is really a euphemism for two much more common euphemisms that have echoed in the ears of girls for generations: "Is it safe?" and "Are you prepared?"

Even the word "responsible" was considered too strong a dose of reality by the NBC network censors. Ralph Daniel, vice president of broadcast standards, said the network wanted the act to be "spontaneous." In a statement that might have come straight through the looking glass, Daniel explained that "our concern was that the series didn't appear to be condoning a sex experience without consequences. The day after the young people go to bed, they begin to worry about pregnancy, and they find that there is an emotional distance between them. The early euphoria is gone, and they experience worry and remorse. That becomes their punishment."

This episode would be funny if it did not epitomize the callousness and irrationality that have hampered the development of a reasonable public policy toward the people who suffer most from "spontaneous" sex— teen-aged girls and the babies they bear. There is an obvious philosophical connection between a network executive who finds it necessary for teen-agers to suffer the "punishment" of worrying about pregnancy and congressmen who cut off Medicaid funds for abortions.

Sunday is the fifth anniversary of the Supreme Court decision legalizing abortion, and I find the occasion a sad reminder of the high hopes for more humane and rational policies that accompanied the case. Like most women in their thirties and forties (public-opinion polls show that women over fifty have more negative attitudes about abortion), I was relieved by the decision and especially hopeful about its impact on the young.

Five years ago, I could never have believed that a craven Congress, under pressure from a well-organized and well-financed minority, would have effectively removed the right to abortion from girls who are young and/or poor. Even when a girl comes from a well-off family, being young in this society usually means being poor in terms of ready access to cash.

I recently interviewed an official in the Department

of Health, Education, and Welfare who advanced the proposition that no one is too poor to raise $175 for a clinic abortion. He is wrong. One of the worst memories of my life concerns an attempt to raise the fairly modest sum of $300 for a friend who needed an illegal abortion when we were both seventeen. I was able to help only because I had a job as a newspaper reporter that paid me an unusual amount of money for a teenager.

While I was waiting for my friend to emerge from the abortionist's office, I saw another girl turned away because she had only $200. She begged to be allowed to raise the additional $100 after the abortion, but the abortionist's assistant said no. I have often wondered what happened to that girl, as I now wonder what will happen to young girls who can no longer obtain abortions at free clinics.

At the time of the Supreme Court decision, I believed that abortion was settled as a legal and a political issue and that the demand for abortions would be greatly reduced within the next few years by effective, sensible contraceptive and sex education programs for teen-agers. I was, of course, wrong on all counts. I had not reckoned with the power of people who are unwilling to face the reality that teen-agers of all races and family backgrounds are having sex and having it at an earlier age than the children of previous generations.

In 1977, girls between ages ten and eighteen gave birth to about 250,000 babies. (More than 13,000 of the births were to girls under fourteen.) An overwhelming majority of these girls are unmarried and incapable of earning a living. They run a much greater risk of dying in childbirth than women in their twenties, and their babies run a much greater risk of serious birth defects or of dying in the first year of life. The birth rate has risen for girls in this age group, while it has fallen for young women above age seventeen.

The silly imbroglio over "James at 15" is all too typical of the attitudes that have contributed to the steady rise in teen-age pregnancies during the 1970's. In Fairfax County, Virginia, an affluent suburb of Washington, the school board finally approved a controversial "sex education" program—with the provision that any discussion of contraception and venereal disease be forbidden.

"There's a big myth that sex education doesn't work, that it doesn't have any impact on the behavior of kids," says Dr. Marlene Hendricks, medical director of a highly regarded youth center in Manhattan called The Door for Alternatives. "In the cases where sex education doesn't work, it's for the same reason any education doesn't work—there's something wrong with the way the subject is being taught. When people want to avoid the subject of sex, of course sex education won't work."

Insofar as public policy is confused rather than callous, it certainly reflects the private confusion of Americans about sex. I recently had a dramatic indication of this in my own life when the sixteen-year-old daughter of a friend came to me and asked me to take her to the doctor for a diaphragm. My first reaction was a flat "You're too young." My second reaction was "If you're really old enough to have sex, why didn't you just go to the doctor by yourself?"

Then I thought about my first visit to a gynecologist at the age of eighteen. There was no sympathetic adult in my life and I had to lie and say I was engaged in order to get birth-control pills. The doctor asked me pointed questions about my intended wedding date and made it clear he thought I was a tramp.

How could I possibly condemn my daughter, or anyone else's daughter, to going through the initiation rites into womanhood in the same loneliness and fear that I did? I couldn't, because I am a woman who remembers what it was like to be a girl.

But I did forget the way it was—if only for a moment—in my knee-jerk reaction that eighteen, and not sixteen, was the proper age for a girl to begin her sex life. If I could forget, it is easy to see the magnitude of the task women face in trying to change the minds of men like President Carter and H.E.W. Secretary Joseph Califano. But it is a task we must accomplish, through political pressure and private persuasion, unless we want the continuation of public policies that promote "punishment" and "remorse" as the proper response to teen-age sex. Because the punishment is greater than young women can bear.

—January 1978

Old and Female: An Economic View

READERS TEND TO SNICKER at newspaper stories with quotations attributed to taxi drivers, because the anonymous "cab driver quote" is a device much favored by reporters who are too lazy to ask any real people for their opinions. But I swear that the following story is an account of a real conversation with a real New York cabby.

He was a talkative widower of sixty-eight with an unsentimental view of relations between men and women. In the fifteen minutes of driving time between La Guardia Airport and my home, he told me exactly why older women get a raw deal in this society.

"I'm no prize to look at, right?" (Right. He had a paunch, thinning hair, and bad teeth.) "I tell you in all honesty that I could have remarried at least a dozen times in the last five years. But I don't want to. I like going out a few times a week, enjoying myself, maybe staying over with a lady on a Saturday night. The women I take out are all in their forties and they look good."

I asked if he ever went out with women his own age.

"Never. You think that's unfair, right? Well, it is unfair. I don't want to go out with women in their sixties. I'll tell you why—their bodies are just as flabby as mine. And, see, I don't have to settle for that. I got a good pension from twenty-five years in the fire department on top of what I make driving a cab. Gives me something to offer a younger woman. Oh, I know they aren't going out with me because I'm so sexy-looking. A woman my age is in a tougher spot. See, she looks just as old as I look, but most of the time she's got no money and no job. The way I figure it, you gotta have something else to offer when the body starts falling apart. Right?"

I see older women everywhere these days—I never really looked at them when I was in my twenties—and their loneliness chills me. A letter from Florida chronicles the sterility of life in a condominium with "1,500 other single women." A widow in my building returns at least one food purchase to the grocery store each day; the clerks are sympathetic, because they understand that she desperately needs the extra minutes of human contact. As for the women I know best—my mother-in-law and grandmother, whose husbands have been dead several years; a friend whose long-time lover died of a heart attack—I can hardly confront their sense of loss.

Sooner or later, their aloneness will be mine. As a woman who loves men—the sight and touch and sound of them, and the fights I have with them—I dread the thought of growing old as I dread nothing else.

I can hear some feminists pointing out that there are many women who choose to live without men and manage to do so quite happily. But each decade of life removes the free choice from more women. Men die younger; one out of every six American women over the age of twenty-one is a widow. The divorce rate has increased most dramatically among couples married twenty to thirty years, and the tendency of men to seek out younger women means that a wife—even when she wants a divorce—is much less likely to find a new partner than her husband is.

It is often assumed that older women are at a disadvantage simply because their bodies are less appealing than those of younger women, but this notion encompasses only a part of the truth. On the crudest level, my taxi driver was saying that you need money to buy love if you haven't got your youth and your looks (regardless of whether you are a woman or a man). On a more sophisticated level, he was saying that money and a job he happened to like—driving a cab and talking his head off—conferred a sense of worth, in his own estimation and in the estimation of women. This sense of worth offset the sexual debit of his expanding paunch.

However cold this equation may seem, it holds out hope for women who do not want to grow old without men. There is nothing that the feminist movement, or any other social movement, can do about aging bodies, but there is a good deal to be done about the lack of worldly esteem that makes middle and old age so bitter for so many women.

Many women complain that "everyone thinks a forty-year-old man is gorgeous, while a forty-year-old woman is considered over the hill." I wonder if everyone, or anyone, really thinks that forty-year-old men are "gorgeous" in comparison to forty-year-old women. Is a man's bald head any more attractive than a woman's graying one? Is a man's potbelly sexier than a woman's flabby thighs? Does anyone who looks at other human beings seriously doubt that the slow process of physical decay begins at about age twenty-five in both sexes?

What is sexy about middle-aged men is not their gorgeous physiques but the worldly accomplishments and status that are, for many women, more of an aphrodisiac than the firm flesh of youth. Society is ordered so that men in their forties and fifties are at the peak of their professional competence and influence and earning power. If similar possibilities were open to more women, there is no doubt in my mind that more men would become interested in sexual partners closer to their own age.

I am not enough of a Marxist to think that improvements in the economic status of older women will render men insensible to the sight of a twenty-one-year-old in a size 8 bikini. But I am not enough of a romantic to think that money—or the lack of it—plays no role in the mystery known as sex appeal.

For millions of women, being left without a man means being reduced to a niggardly standard of living that could hardly enhance anyone's sexual attractiveness. Six out of ten American widows live below the official poverty line. In *The Economics of Being a Woman* (Macmillan), Dee Dee Ahern and Betsy Bliss point out that only 2 per cent of widows are receiving private pension benefits from their spouses' working years. The average private pension for retired women in 1976 was only $81 a month.

Small wonder, then, that my sixty-eight-year-old cab driver prefers forty-year-old women to sixty-five-year-old women. He not only gets a younger body—he also gets a woman who is capable of earning her own living.

No amount of money or achievement can compensate for the loss of a beloved man, and no improvement in the overall status of women can nullify the mortality tables decreeing that most of us will spend the closing years of our lives without a man. But I do think that a woman with substantial economic and professional assets is less likely to be passed over for someone twenty or thirty years younger. As the man said, "You gotta have something else to offer when the body starts falling apart."

—*March 1978*

When a good many readers miss a writer's point (as opposed to disagreeing with it), there are two possibilities: The article is unclear or the writer has hit a nerve that makes it too painful for readers to confront the issue directly. What I said in this column was that financial independence enhances a woman's (or a man's) sex appeal and that the lack of financial independence is one factor in the sexual and social loneliness of many older women. Some readers misinterpreted this observation as a statement that the main reason women should attain economic self-sufficiency is to catch a man.

One woman wrote:

The conclusion . . . that women should develop their potential is just fine, but the reasoning is horrifying. Even if one accepts the assumption that a rich old woman is more desirable to a man than a poor old woman, how can anyone who argues on behalf of a new social view of women state such a view?

"When she describes elderly widows living in the midst of others like themselves as 'alone,' she is sharing the devaluation of women that is the hallmark of our sexist society. On what other basis can being with women be defined as being 'alone'?"

Another woman, in a much angrier letter, said:

"I had to go back and read the 'Hers' article of today a second time. Sure enough, right there in the opening portion, the taxi driver states he could have married several times in the past years *but he doesn't want to*. If being well-off financially means being more 'attractive' sexually to such a man, what might an older woman expect from such a relationship?

"I will be fifty years old soon. I *am* well off financially (though admittedly with some obligations with two children still to educate)—but those are obligations I choose to bear. Why would I want to use my money to attract a man who doesn't find me attractive *personally* or want to marry again in any case? I don't need any male prostitutes, thank you! The only reason I can see for an older woman to want to attract a man might be to escape financial burdens—but if the man doesn't care enough about her to take them on, or make a real commitment to her as a person by marrying, why bother with him?

"Anyway, if one of those forty-year-old women succeeds in 'catching' some sixty-plus man, she may very well find herself spending months or perhaps years caring for an invalided, sickly man and wearing herself out physically at the same time—which may very well have been his ulterior motive in marrying her in the first place. Who needs it? If sincere love doesn't exist on both sides, the price of male companionship comes too high."

A third reader simply said:

"It is simply revolting to speak of love and money in the same breath. At any age, we want to be loved for ourselves alone."

All of these letters displayed an interesting confusion between being "rich" and being "economically independent." A male taxi driver with a fireman's pension is not "rich," but he is able to live decently. The ability to live in ordinary comfort, either on the basis of current earnings or pensions accumulated from work before retirement, is precisely what so many older women lack.

The letters also demonstrate the polite unease so many women display when they attempt to confront questions of money. Being loved for "ourselves alone" is a notion appropriate to teen-agers. The adult "self" is the sum of many qualities, which include traits of character and intelligence as well as physical appearance. The ability to earn one's own living is, it seems to me, no less lovable a trait than loyalty or kindness or a warm smile.

Getting Off the Dole

MY GRANDMOTHER is a great lady who has always known the value of a dollar. Born into a family of German immigrants at the turn of the century, she began working as an onion picker when she was a child. She never finished high school; when her family needed money, she pitched in and found a job operating an office calculator.

At nineteen, Gran became a bride. My grandfather was very handsome, very Irish, and very old-fashioned in his ideas about how money should be managed in a marriage. He made the money, he paid the bills, and he

gave his wife an allowance. I doubt that my grandmother ever knew exactly how much her husband
earned, but she always kept a close rein on her household expenditures. Grandpa was generous to the point
of being a spendthrift, and he frequently teased Gran
about the frugality that was a result of her childhood.
When he was dying, one of his chief worries was
whether my grandmother would be able to manage her
finances after more than fifty years of marriage.

"That was really the last thing he should have worried about," Gran says today with a small chuckle. "I
was always pretty good at math, and I keep that check-
book in good order. I have a feeling I'm more careful
about paying the bills on time than Gramps was. Things
were different when we were young—money was the
man's business alone."

I am, so I am told, the child of a more liberated era.
I worked my way through college as a newspaper reporter and have made my living as a writer ever since.
No one else handles my bills or writes my checks; married or single, I pay my own way. Nevertheless, my attitudes about some of the most important financial matters affecting my life have had more in common with
the ideas of my grandmother's generation than I was
once willing to admit.

When I married seven years ago, I didn't even bother
to maintain the charge accounts I had established as a
single working woman. I quietly submitted when stores
informed me that I would have to reapply for credit in
my husband's name, on the basis of his income. More
significantly, I turned over most of the long-range decisions about money—decisions that could shape the rest
of my life—to my husband. On second thought,
"turned over" is not the right expression to describe my
behavior: I dumped the decisions in his lap. Unlike my
grandfather, my husband never requested or demanded
the job of handling our finances. But I expected him to
deal with the taxes, insurance, pension plans, investments—all of the important, detailed, and sometimes
dull money problems that are part of everyone's life.
When I made a suggestion, I would expect him to do

the work of carrying it out. I might mention that we ought to set up our own pension plans because we were both self-employed. He would say fine, great, he would look into it. A month later, I would ask where the information was. He would say he hadn't had time to do anything about it. I would never volunteer to "look into it" myself and he would never ask me to take over. Why? Because—well, because money was the man's business.

I was married nearly five years before I realized that I had abdicated my financial identity. It took me the better part of a year to re-establish my individual credit standing by opening bank and charge accounts and obtaining major credit cards in my maiden (also my professional) name. During that year, when I spent a considerable amount of time fighting *apparatchiks* who had never heard of laws forbidding sex discrimination in lending, I came to the conclusion that I had been my own worst enemy. My reluctance to take on the adult responsibility of managing my own money was rooted in attitudes handed down from generation to generation—attitudes that have even less relationship to reality today than they did when my grandmother was a young woman. Yet I believe these ideas are shared to one degree or another by most women—regardless of age, marital status, or how much money they make.

The most damaging gender-related attitudes about money are instilled during childhood:

It isn't polite or ladylike to talk about money.
Girls can't handle finances because they aren't good at math.
You'll find a good man to take care of all that for you.

To some extent, both boys and girls are inculcated with the idea that it is slightly vulgar to raise questions about money. For girls, the message is reinforced by the fear that they will be considered unfeminine if they seem to know anything about the mysteries of high and low finance. I suspect that the polite secrecy surrounding money is even more prevalent in middle-class homes today than it was in poorer households when my grandmother was a girl. Poor people—and most of our immigrant ancestors were poor—cannot afford the luxury of genteel diffidence about money.

False politeness handicaps women in all of their financial dealings and reinforces economic discrimination. I have noticed that men and women behave quite differently when they ask their employers for raises. Most men consider their need for more money as a purely pragmatic matter; they ask themselves if the timing is right and what they will do if they are turned down. But many women are afraid they will be considered "pushy" if they ask for a raise. "I want people to pay me what I'm worth without having to ask," a friend once told me after she had been working at a foundation for two years at the same salary. She was unable to recognize the fact that most employers will pay anyone—male or female—as little as possible if they think the person is too insecure to demand a raise. Reticence won't pay a woman's bills.

Probably the most significant fallacy underlying women's financial behavior is the notion that some man will come along and "take care of all that." No matter that more women are staying single or marrying at a later age. No matter that female participation in the labor force increases each year and that the income of working wives is vital to their families. No matter that more than seven million families are headed by women. No matter that the spiraling divorce rate and the gap in life expectancy between men and women means that nearly every woman will have to take care of herself and/or her children at some point in her life. We still cling to the fantasy that some man will always be around to shield us from the impolite, unfeminine realities of economic life.

It is a fantasy for which women can pay dearly. Lynn Caine, in a book simply titled *Widow* (Morrow, New York, 1974), describes the "craziness" about money that temporarily paralyzed her after her husband died and left her with two young children to support.

"One bizarre caper of mine was to write a rich politician:

'You are fat and rich; I am poor and thin. My husband died leaving me with no life insurance and two small children to support on a publishing salary. Would you please send me $500,000.

'I met you at a literary cocktail party in Washington and you drove me to the airport.

'I look forward to hearing from you.' "

A woman does not need to be a widow to recognize the danger of relying on someone else to solve her money problems. My husband and I have nearly equal incomes, but I realized only recently that I should have disability insurance to provide me with some money in the event of an illness or injury. My husband does have disability insurance, but our former insurance agent never suggested the obvious—that we should both have insurance because our standard of living depends on both of our incomes.

When I came to him to buy insurance, he shook his head dubiously and tried to discourage me. "It costs a lot," he said, "and your need isn't really that acute."

"What do you mean, my need isn't acute," I said. "If I landed in the hospital for three months, half of our income would go down the drain."

"Half?" he asked incredulously.

"Half," I answered firmly.

To be sure, the insurance agent was at fault for acting on old stereotypes about women and for failing to realize that a woman's income can be as essential to her family as a man's. But that is the way most insurance agents and bank officers and employers are. Their attitudes and discriminatory practices can only be changed by women who are willing to grow up and stop behaving like children with play money. In emotion, if not in fact, too many of us are still living on the dole.

—November 1976

Three Generations, Two Women, One Roof

ONE OF THE MANY MATTERS in which there has been no women's liberation is the responsibility for aging parents who can no longer live alone. The care of the old, like the care of the young, is woman's work.

"Nine times out of ten, it's the daughter rather than the son who comes to us for help," says Daphne H. Krause, a pioneer in community efforts to keep old men and women independent and out of institutions. She is the head of the Minneapolis Age and Opportunity Center, a program which offers nearly every imaginable form of aid, from hot meals delivered at home to transportation to the doctor, to the old and to middle-aged children who want their parents to remain as self-sufficient as possible.

"The degree to which people in this country 'abandon' their parents is greatly exaggerated," says Krause. "What you do have, what I see every day, are people in their forties, torn between their obligations to their parents and to their teen-aged children who are about to enter college—a situation which places a maximum financial burden on the family. But this whole conflict cuts much deeper for women than for men, because women have a very broad sense of obligation connected with being a 'good daughter'—just as they do with being a 'good mother.' A man will frequently feel he has discharged his obligation by helping his parents out financially. It's usually the woman who deals with the day-to-day human problems, juggling responsibilities to different generations."

The "human problem" which seems to inspire the

most fear in middle-aged adults is the prospect of deciding whether to put a sick parent in a nursing home. The justified publicity surrounding nursing-home scandals has made this seem to be a more common problem than it actually is. Most old people—fortunately for themselves and their families—remain in good enough health to stay out of institutions. Fewer than 5 per cent of Americans over the age of sixty-five live in any type of institution; the largest proportion of nursing-home residents are above age eighty.

A far more common dilemma confronts families with parents who find it increasingly difficult to live alone because of chronic health problems, lack of money, the deterioration of a once-comfortable old neighborhood, or acute loneliness after the death of a husband or wife. For these families, there are really only two choices: They can provide their parents with the kind of emotional support and financial aid that will enable them to remain on their own, or they can invite their parents to move in with them.

The three-generation household has not (as one might think from reading endless reports on the disintegration of the American family) gone the way of the horse and buggy. A significant minority of the old— about one third of all men and women over the age of sixty-five who do not have living spouses—make their homes with their adult children.

A home with parents, children, and grandchildren is not entirely satisfactory from the standpoint of any of the three generations, but it is a way of life that has been tried by millions of Americans who are searching for the difficult problem of how to help their parents without disrupting their own lives.

Because the average American wife outlives her husband by six to ten years, most old people left alone are women. Three-generation households usually include a widowed mother, a middle-aged daughter and her husband, and their children. Few women move in with their son's rather than their daughter's families. Thus, the quality of life in a three-generation home depends primarily on the relationship between a daughter in her forties or fifties and a mother in her sixties or seventies.

In all of the families I visited, husbands and wives agreed that it is the middle-aged woman who bears the brunt of adjustment problems in a three-generation household.

In the home of Gail and David Thayer of Bergen, New Jersey, I found a classic example of what can go wrong when a mother and daughter—in spite of their best intentions—are still playing out the scenes and recriminations of twenty or thirty years ago. The Thayer family abandoned the experiment in three-generation living after two years of conflict, mainly because of bitter disagreements between the two women over the upbringing of the family's teen-aged children. "I found I was holding back an enormous amount of anger, just as I did when I was a little girl," explained Gail Thayer, a thin, dark-haired woman in her late forties. "There's one important piece of advice I have for people in this situation. That is—remember how it was with your parents when you were growing up. If you have a lot of unresolved conflicts left over from that time, it's going to be worse when you're older."

Until her husband died five years ago, Gail Thayer's mother, Angela Peretti, lived contentedly in the neighborhood in Newark, New Jersey, where she had spent all of her married life. It had become a high-crime neighborhood, but that did not matter to Mrs. Peretti as long as her husband was alive.

"Everything changed when Dad died," Gail Thayer remembers. "Mom was scared. Someone broke into her house. Then she was mugged on the street on her way home from the grocery store. She fell down and broke her leg. At that point, we felt we had to do something."

The Thayers considered the possibility of paying the rent on an apartment in a safer neighborhood, but rejected it mainly because they did not have the extra money. "I was the one who really said, 'Why not invite her to move in with us?'" David Thayer acknowledges. "I've always been very fond of Gail's mother, and I really didn't think about the whole problem of the two women getting along. I wasn't the one who was going to be home all day."

The Thayers were concerned enough about privacy to build a room with a separate entrance and bath over their garage.

"We thought it would protect our privacy and Mom's," says Gail with a rueful smile. "We moved Mom's things in on a Saturday, and the first fight was at eight o'clock Sunday morning. Mom appeared in the kitchen—she was still on crutches—and asked which mass we were going to. She's gone to mass every Sunday all her life. I know it, but I just hadn't thought about it. Dave isn't a Catholic, and I only go to church on Christmas and Easter. Mom hadn't known that about me. But the thing that really made her furious was we didn't make the kids go to church either. I remember Mom saying, 'You can live any way you want to, miss, but you shouldn't be bringing up your children with no religion.' That was just the beginning."

The Thayer children, Tom and Julie, were twelve and fourteen years old when their grandmother came to live with them. Julie was to become the major source of conflict between Gail Thayer and her mother. Gail started to sketch the situation and then changed her mind: "Maybe I should let Julie tell you about it herself." Julie, now seventeen, immediately appeared from the den, where she had been doing her homework and listening to the interview.

"When Grandma came to live with us, I was a freshman in high school and I was being allowed to go out on dates for the first time. A lot of my friends started dating when they were in junior high, but Mom and Dad said I had to wait until I was in high school."

"Anyway, it drove Grandma up the wall that I was allowed to go out alone with boys. She and Mom were fighting about it all the time—once she even told Mom if I started out this early I'd wind up pregnant. The thing is, my parents are strict by the standards of a lot of my friends. There was a rule that I had to be home an hour after a dance or a movie ended, unless it was something really special like a prom. One night I pulled into the driveway at midnight, and my date and I sat in the car—no longer than ten minutes.

"Then suddenly the light goes on over the garage and Grandma comes down. She opens the car door, pulls me out, screams at my date. I thought, wow, she's treating me like I'm her daughter and she has the right to make the rules!" Julie smiled at her mother. "You know, one thing I got out of all that was a lot better understanding of Mom. I mean, I saw what it was like for her to be a daughter instead of a mother. You only think of your parents as your parents—you never think that they've had a whole life long before you were ever on the scene."

Gail Thayer kissed her daughter on the cheek. "You know," she said, "Julie's right about that. Tom was too young to feel anything except that there was a lot of tension, but Julie really grew up and we became much closer. It was an experience that did enable her to see her parents, especially me, as human beings. But I didn't like what was developing—a kind of alliance of her and me against my mother. It wasn't a healthy thing."

The incident that finally triggered the Thayers' decision to break up their three-generation household involved not their daughter but their son. "Tommy is a diabetic," Mrs. Thayer explained. "He has to have insulin and he absolutely can't eat sweets. Now, this is a constant battle with a child. The doctor explained to us that diabetic children are often ashamed to admit something is wrong with them, and they do things like going off their diet just to prove they're like everybody else. We explained all that to Mom.

"One day we came home and found Tommy calmly sitting in the kitchen and eating chocolate-chip cookies. Mom had baked them. Dave yelled at Tommy, going on about the possibility of a diabetic coma. He simply said, 'Grandma told me it would be all right just this once.' So there we were. In a situation involving a child's life, our authority was being challenged."

Once Gail and David Thayer had agreed they could no longer live with Mrs. Peretti, they faced the old problem of what to do next. "She couldn't go back to the old neighborhood in Newark, because the house had been sold," David Thayer says. "Besides, all of her old friends had either died or left. But there was still the money problem. Two years had passed, Julie was getting closer to college age, and we still didn't have the money to afford a separate place for Gail's mother."

The problem was solved when Gail decided to brush up on her secretarial skills and return to work for the first time in sixteen years. "I'd been thinking about going back to work for a long time, and this seemed like a good point to do it. We didn't need a housekeeper—the kids were old enough to be alone after school. And my salary would give us the extra money we needed to help Mom on the rent for an apartment."

She expected a terrible scene when she told her mother about her decision but was pleasantly surprised at the reaction she received. "Mom was relieved," she remembers. "She said she had always been used to being the mistress of her own house and this had been as hard on her as on us." Mrs. Peretti now lives in an apartment complex a half-hour's drive from her daughter, and she sees her children and grandchildren once a week—under more pleasant circumstances than she did while they were living together. The energy she once devoted to interfering with her grandchildren's lives is now spent on volunteer church work.

"What was really wrong," Gail Thayer observed thoughtfully, "was that our lives were completely different from Mom's old life. She didn't have any of the things she had to occupy her time in her old neighborhood, so she got much more involved with our lives than she would have otherwise."

Although Gail Thayer is aware that everyone in the family is happier with her mother living in her own apartment, she still feels she is violating her own image of a "good daughter."

"I have this idea of what a good daughter is," she says, "and it's what my own mother was to her mother. Sacrificing all the time to serve others. This image also has a lot in common with what I used to think of as being a 'good mother.' "

When I spoke to Mrs. Peretti, I was interested to find that her account of the preceding two years was essentially the same as her daughter's. "My Gayla *is* a good daughter," she said fiercely. "She goes to work so she can help me pay for this apartment. Maybe I would have done the same if I had the chance when my mama was left alone. I didn't know how to do anything—I only finished five grades of school. Gayla doesn't remember how my mama and I used to fight. She was born in the old country, she never wanted me to let my daughter go out with a boy alone at all. Oh, it's not so different, the fights Gayla and I have. But back when I was young, there was no choice. Your mama was left alone, she came to live with you."

The conflict in the Thayers' experience might seem to be an entirely predictable result of three-generation living, but I found many other families with smoother histories. These were families in which the mother and daughter had always had a comfortable relationship—and they were families in which the values of the older and the middle-aged generations were essentially the same.

Shirley and Jerome Shapiro of Wantagh, New York, have lived with their eleven-year-old son and Mrs. Shapiro's seventy-six-year-old mother for many years. Like Gail Thayer, Shirley Shapiro had disagreements with her mother about child rearing. Unlike Mrs. Thayer, she was able to confront her mother directly when she felt her authority was being eroded. "Mom and I have always been able to talk things out," she says. "If we were the sort of people who held things in, we couldn't possibly live under the same roof. No one in this family has ever been scared of a good argument."

Like the Thayers—and like most people who invite a parent to live with them—the Shapiros had moved from their old neighborhood in the city to a newer one in the suburbs when they asked Mrs. Shapiro's mother,

Mildred Moses, to move in with them. Like Mrs. Peretti, Mrs. Moses had lost her husband and was experiencing serious money problems because of repeated rent increases by her landlord.

But the resemblance between the Thayers and the Shapiros ends there. Mildred Moses was intimately involved with her daughter's family long before they moved into the same house, and she got along well with her daughter, son-in-law, and grandchildren.

"If you never got along with your parents when you were younger, there isn't any way you'll get along when you're in your forties and they're in their sixties," says Shirley Shapiro, a forthright woman who looks a decade younger than her fifty-six years. "People just don't change that much."

Mrs. Shapiro explained that her family, including her brother and sister-in-law, had always been unusually close and became even more so when the Shapiros' daughter died of cancer several years ago.

"My mom was a help in every way during the long months and years when our daughter was sick," she said. "I don't know how I could have gotten through it without her."

"Oh, no, you don't want to talk about that," her mother interrupted.

"It's important, Mom," Mrs. Shapiro replied firmly. "It had a lot of influence on what our family is like now." Turning toward me and ruffling her son Mark's blond hair, she went on with her story.

"Before my daughter got sick I had a job as a dental technician, but I had to give that up because someone had to be home all the time. Jerry was working incredibly long hours, because, of course, our health insurance wasn't paying for all of the treatment our daughter needed. At a time like that, you appreciate what a family means if you didn't appreciate it before. My daughter would have to make the long trip on the subway from Brooklyn to the hospital in Manhattan for chemotherapy, and either Mom or I would go with her. In all that time she never had to make the trip alone. A tragedy like that can either break a family apart—each person going off into his own grief—or it can bring a family closer together. In our case, we came closer to each other. And during all that time while my mom was helping me, she was going through her own grief because my father had recently died."

The Shapiros do not believe in keeping secrets from children. Mark, who asked to be present because he wanted to find out what an interview was, had obviously heard the story many times. He also knows he was adopted after the Shapiros' daughter died.

"We'd just about given up on being able to find a baby to adopt," Mrs. Shapiro remembers. "We'd already moved out to Long Island, and then our old rabbi in Brooklyn was able to help us find Mark. It never occurred to us *not* to tell Mark he was adopted. After all, Jerry and I are older than most parents of kids his age, and he would have figured it out when he got older anyway."

"I was *picked*," Mark interrupted.

"You sure were," his grandmother replied, shaking her head because Mark had roped himself to the banister in imitation of a television show called "Spiderman." "The only thing we didn't know was about all these rope tricks you'd learn to do."

When Mrs. Moses moved in with the Shapiros eleven years ago, the family had not anticipated the arrival of a small child. Their older son, now twenty-nine, had already started college when his parents moved to Long Island. Both Mrs. Shapiro and her mother agreed that children provide the greatest potential for conflict in a three-generation home.

"First of all," Shirley Shapiro says, "having both parents and grandparents in a house probably means that a child is spoiled more than usual. We had to work that out in the early years—Mark was an especially beloved and wanted child because our older son was already away from home and because of the loss we had suffered."

For Mrs. Shapiro, the major problem of raising a

child in a three-generation household stemmed not from differing philosophies of child rearing but from the desire of two women to exert their authority in one home.

"When Mark was younger, we'd both be telling him what to do at once. It wasn't necessarily that we had different ideas, but we were both giving orders. That can confuse a child. But we just settled it. I spoke very frankly to Mom and to Mark, and made it clear that Jerry and I were the authorities when we are at home. If neither of us is home and something comes up, then Mark knows he's supposed to listen to his grandmother. It's very important for a child to know who has the final responsibility, the final authority in his life. But it never got to be a very serious problem with us. Mom and I have just always been able to talk things out, and it isn't any different now than when we were younger."

If child rearing can cause conflict in a three-generation home, it can also be a source of pleasure to children and grandparents. Jerry Shapiro, who never knew his own grandparents because they remained behind in Russia when his parents immigrated to the United States, is convinced that children who have a close relationship with their grandparents are better off than those who don't.

Mark is too young to take much of an interest in family history, but his fifteen-year-old cousin often drops by to prod his grandmother for family memories. Mrs. Moses takes considerable pride in her role as a family historian.

"I'm the only one who knows all the things my grandson—that is, Mark's cousin—wants to know. I'm the only one who's old enough. I think for some reason the kids today are more interested in this kind of thing than they were ten years ago. I don't know. Maybe it's the influence of 'Roots.' I've started to remember things I had forgotten for years."

At seventy-six, Mildred Moses is the product of a generation in which young members of a family were expected to take considerable responsibility for older relatives. She raised her own children in that tradition, but she is keenly aware of the painful new problems that can arise when a healthy old person becomes seriously ill. Some years ago, Mrs. Moses and Mrs. Shapiro shared the burden of caring for a relative who was in her nineties. They eventually were forced to place her in a nursing home.

"It became too much in this house with no outside help and one bathroom," Mrs. Moses remembers. "You feel very guilty, very sad about it . . . when you have to put a relative in a nursing home. But there comes a point where someone is so sick that normal family life is completely disrupted. When a person can't use the bathroom, can't dress herself, can't go up and down stairs, then you have to ask yourself what it's doing to the rest of the family. I wouldn't ever like to feel that I was that kind of a burden."

Both Mrs. Moses and the Shapiros describe life in a three-generation home as a continuing series of compromises.

"I'm sure Shirley and Jerry would like to have the house to themselves," Mrs. Moses says. "You sacrifice a lot in privacy when you have a parent living with you. The feelings of warmth and family love aren't something you can measure so easily."

I asked the Shapiros whether they would want to live with their children when they were older.

"I don't think that's going to happen," said Shirley Shapiro with a slow smile. "For right or wrong, people my age brought up their children to be more selfish."

Jerry Shapiro said bluntly, "I wouldn't want to live with my children. Everyone would prefer to be self-sufficient." Mrs. Moses nodded her head in agreement. "But," Jerry continued, "life doesn't always give you what you want. You don't always know whether you're going to have enough money to make it on your own and, more important, the good health to enjoy it. We're talking about a problem—what happens when a person gets old—in a world that isn't ideal. So you come up with the best solution you can, and it isn't ideal either."

I asked Shirley Shapiro if she felt the care of the old was "woman's work."

"Yes, yes, I suppose I do," she replied. "I'm a traditional woman in that way, like my mother. And I agree that everyone would rather be independent. But it's as Jerry says—this isn't an ideal world, everyone doesn't stay independent until death. I feel uncomfortable when I hear a lot of talk about how women should feel less responsible for others. What is right, it seems to me, is that a boy should be raised to feel *more* responsible."

—April 1978

No Special Service—Just a Little Equality, Please

ROSALYN S. YALOW, winner of the 1977 Nobel Prize in Medicine, stood up at the end of a formal banquet in Stockholm and told her fellow Nobel laureates some truths about the status of women—truths seldom spoken by a woman of unquestionable authority before a group of male luminaries.

"We still live in a world," Yalow said, "in which a significant fraction of people, including women, believe that a woman belongs and wants to belong exclusively in the home, that a woman should not aspire to achieve more than her male counterparts, and particularly not more than her husband." Since the announcement of her Nobel award, Yalow has repeatedly made it clear that she is not in favor of "reverse discrimination" for women. What women need, she says, is the equal opportunity they have not yet achieved.

All of this blunt talk—coming from a renowned scientist who had to go to work as a secretary when she graduated from college because she was told a woman would never be admitted to graduate school in physics—provides a much-needed corrective to the idea that women have not only achieved equal opportunity but are now receiving special favor at the expense of downtrodden white men.

This notion is nonsense.

It is, unfortunately, the sort of nonsense that threatens the limited, hard-won gains women have achieved since the mid-1960's. In spite of the well-publicized advances of a minority of women in business, government, law, medicine, and journalism, there has been no basic change in the inferior position of most women in relation to men in the job market. The salary gap between full-time men and women workers has widened during the last decade; millions of women have now entered the labor force, but they are still concentrated in poorly paid clerical and service jobs. Only a few of us, baby, have come a long way.

Nothing has done more to confuse the issue of "reverse discrimination" as it relates to women than the Allan Bakke case. Bakke, a white man whose case is now before the Supreme Court, claims he was unfairly refused admission to the University of California, Davis School of Medicine because a number of places were reserved for black and Hispanic students with lower entrance test scores.* Newspaper articles and television reports invariably describe the Bakke case as a

---

* The Supreme Court handed down a complicated decision in the Bakke case on June 28, 1978. By a 5–4 decision, the Court ordered Bakke admitted to medical school because the Davis program was based on an inflexible quota that excluded whites. By another 5–4 vote, however, the Court upheld the constitutionality of "affirmative action" programs designed to compensate for past discrimination against blacks and other minorities—as long as those programs do not contain rigid quotas.

For women, a more significant action came the following week in a ruling on an employment case. The justice refused to review a lower court ruling upholding the American Telephone and Telegraph Company's affirmative action program. Unlike most affirmative action programs in universities, the A T & T plan does affect women as well as black and Hispanic workers. It has been used as a model by smaller companies across the country, and a successful legal challenge would have been an incalculable defeat for the women's movement and for minority groups.

test of programs designed to expand educational and employment opportunities for "blacks, women and other minorities."

Classifying women with blacks and "other minorities" is a vast oversimplification of a complex issue. On the one hand, this viewpoint insults women (and blacks) by assuming they cannot meet the regular admissions standards for graduate and professional schools. On the other hand, it does blacks an injustice by failing to take into account the history of unequal education that makes it hard for them to equal the *group* performance of twenty-one-year-old whites on standardized tests. The American educational system has inflicted two very different kinds of damage on women and blacks. Most blacks were victimized by inferior elementary and secondary schooling from the moment they entered first grade, but girls received essentially the same education as boys in elementary and high schools. The "No Women Need Apply" signs never appeared until a girl wanted to enter a university department or professional school leading to a job that had traditionally been reserved for men.

When graduate and professional schools began opening their doors to women on an equal basis in the early 1970's, women were fully qualified to take advantage of the opportunity. Women score slightly higher than any group in the population on tests for admission to some of the most highly competitive schools in the country.

At Harvard Medical School, for example, 54 out of 165 members of this year's entering class were women. One out of every 25 male applicants and one out of every 20 females was admitted—not because women were given a special break but because the women, as a group, had an edge in academic qualifications. The same pattern is evident in admissions to most law schools.

No doubt there are disappointed male applicants to Harvard who are under the illusion that they were passed over for less qualified women. Hard as it may be for some men to believe, they were turned down for *better* qualified women.

Although the problems of blacks and women are far from identical, the two groups do belong on the same side of "reverse discrimination" suits brought by white men. Most of these suits are based on the principle that there is such a thing as an "objective" standard for educational and career advancement, and that this standard is being violated by programs to expand opportunities for women and blacks.

Unless strict union seniority rules are in force, the idea that hirings and promotions are based only on objective standards is worthy of a belly laugh from both employers and employees. When a young woman or man is looking for a job, employers usually decide not on the basis of "objective" records but on hunches about whether the kid is likely to succeed. Most employers are white men, and their hunches have seldom worked in favor of women and blacks. Even men who want to overcome the old prejudices frequently find it difficult to view prospective men and women employees in the same way.

Last year, I was talking with a Washington newspaper editor for whom I have considerable respect. He said he wanted to hire more women, but added that "most of the good women writers are in New York and don't want to move to Washington." I told him I was sure he could lure some women to Washington if he used the same incentive he would use if he wanted a man—a large salary increase. A silence fell over the office, as if using money to attract a woman were a truly startling business innovation.

On another occasion, a magazine executive asked me if I would like to come to work as an editor. I told him thanks but no thanks, I was a writer. He said ruefully, "Women just don't want to be editors." I find it hard to imagine the same executive, turned down by a man, saying, "Men just don't want to be editors." When you want to hire a man, you go on to another man if you are turned down by your first choice. I suppose if I had taken the job, it would have been perceived as "reverse discrimination," even though the man who was eventually hired had as little editing experience as I did.

When Rosalyn Yalow threw away her steno pads in 1941, after finally being admitted to graduate school in physics, I wonder if anyone said, "Women just don't want to be secretaries."

—*December 1977*

LOOKING
BACK

Women of Letters

In the awful years of the terror I spent seventeen months waiting in line outside the prison in Leningrad. One day somebody in the crowd identified me. Standing behind me was a woman, with lips blue from the cold, who had, of course, never heard me called by name before. Now she emerged from the torpor common to us all and asked me in a whisper (we all whispered there):

"Can you describe this?"

And I said, "I can."

Then something like a smile passed fleetingly over what had once been her face.

Those lines were written by the Russian poet Anna Akhmatova as an introduction to her poem "Requiem," a grim and beautiful lament for the victims of the Stalinist terror in her country. I recently recalled those lines—as one might recall a prayer—in the midst of an interminable, sodden argument over the question of whether there is a "special female sensibility" in literature.

The argument took place at a holiday dinner party filled with the sort of people who don't read books written before 1970. The usual dumb discussion about female sensibility produced an unusually dumb comment from a professor of something-or-other (I hope for the sake of his students that it wasn't history or literature) at Columbia. Women, the professor intoned, have not produced writers who act as "witnesses to history"—no Alexander Solzhenitsyns, for example. Oh, professor, I thought, did you pick the wrong country to prove your point.

There is no law that says genius must be fairly distributed by sex or race or religion or height. As luck would have it, Russian poetic genius in the first half of the twentieth century was parceled out to two women and two men: Anna Akhmatova and Marina Tsvetayeva, Osip Mandelstam and Boris Pasternak. Of the four, only Ahkmatova and Pasternak lived through what has come to be known as "the great terror"; only they survived to encompass the whole story in their art.

Also by terrible chance, this poetic constellation helped produce another great woman writer (or writer who happens to be a woman, take your pick)— Nadezhda Mandelstam, whose husband died somewhere en route to a prison camp in 1938. (Osip Mandelstam's fate was sealed when he wrote a poem describing Stalin as a "murderer and peasant-slayer.") Mrs. Mandelstam, often one step ahead of the secret police, traversed the length and breadth of Russia, preserving her husband's verse in her head lest his manuscripts be destroyed.

Then, when she was already in her sixties, Nadezhda Mandelstam began writing two extraordinary books (published in English under the titles *Hope Against Hope* and *Hope Abandoned*) that resurrected her husband, the culture that produced him, and an entire world of humane and humanistic values that buckled under the weight of sustained totalitarianism. To understand what went on in the camps, you read Solzhenitsyn. To understand what went on in the imprisoned nation outside the camps, you read Akhmatova's poetry and Nadezhda Mandelstam's prose. The two women were fast friends who lived through the same appalling events.

These are the writers I began reading when I lived and worked as a journalist in Moscow in the late 1960's. I was more powerfully drawn to the Russian women than I had ever been to women writers in my own language; I now think the unfamiliar culture made it possible for me to approach writers of my own sex without relegating them to the second-rate categories of "lady writer" or "authoress" or "poetess"—categories I had absorbed in my impressionable youth from men like the professor at the dinner party.

Russians freed me from the musty notion that "manners" and domesticity are the province of women and great external events the province of male writers. There are fear and death and starvation—the stuff of domestic and public trauma—in both Solzhenitsyn and Nadezhda Mandelstam. The angles of vision differ, but both writers are "witnesses to history."

In *Hope Abandoned*, Mrs. Mandelstam (whose husband is referred to as "M.") describes his visit to a Soviet clinic for a physical checkup at some point in the 1920's. He was passed on to a psychiatrist, whose diagnosis "was that M. had the illusion of being a poet and of writing verse, though in fact he was only a minor employee who did not even hold a post of any responsibility and harbored all kinds of grudges, speaking badly, for instance, about writers' organizations. . . . M.'s delusion was, moreover, a very deep one: It was impossible to convince him that he was not a poet. The psychiatrist advised me not to succumb myself to this psychosis . . . and in the future to cut short all my husband's talk about writing verse."

The incident tells us as much about the course of the young Soviet state as it does about the Mandelstams' hounded lives. Mrs. Mandelstam—the writer, the woman—remembers everything. When *Hope Abandoned* was published here in 1974, a feminist writer criticized it on grounds that the author "seemed too preoccupied with her husband." How ironic that a feminist should suggest, as any garden-variety male chauvinist might, that the inescapable vantage point of a brilliant woman whose brilliant husband was murdered somehow disqualified Mrs. Mandelstam as a writer of universal vision. I prefer the interpretation of the Russian émigré poet Joseph Brodsky, who has described Nadezhda Mandelstam's evocation of her husband as "reminiscent of the creation from a rib—with the sexes reversed."

Anna Akhmatova's poetry (some of it is available in English translation) has the same quality of "bearing witness" that permeates her friend's prose. The poetry written around the time of the purges has a tone that is both elegiac and reportorial. "At dawn they came and took you away" begins one of the stanzas in "Requiem."

"At dawn they came and took you away/You were the corpse, I walked behind." That line refers to the arrest of her husband. Her son, Lev Gumilev, was arrested three times while Stalin was alive and was finally released from a labor camp in 1956. The poet writes about all of this. What is "domestic" and what is "public" in the sufferings of a woman, a mother, a child, a country? How do they divide into "male" and "female" subjects?

Of course there is a female sensibility. Of course there is a male sensibility. In a great writer of either sex, those sensibilities yield universal truths. I suspect that all of the dull dinner-party arguments on this point stem from the fact that we read too few great writers and too much junk. In another famous poem, Akhmatova lamented that her life had been wrenched from its normal course by the horrors of the age in which she lived. The verse concludes:

But if I could step outside myself
and contemplate the person that I am,
I would know at last what envy is.

Was it a man or a woman who wrote those lines?

—January 1978

World of Our Mothers

As we come marching, marching in the beauty of the
*   day,*
A million darkened kitchens, a thousand mill lofts gray,
Are touched with all the radiance that a sudden sun
*   discloses,*
For the people hear us singing, "Bread and roses!
*   Bread and roses!"*

As we come marching, marching, we battle too for
*   men,*
For they are women's children, and we mother them
*   again.*
Our lives shall not be sweated from birth until life closes;
Hearts starve as well as bodies; give us bread, but give
*   us roses!*

As we come marching, marching, unnumbered women
*   dead*
Go crying through our singing their ancient cry for
*   bread.*
Small art and love and beauty their drudging spirits
*   knew.*
Yes, it is bread we fight for—but we fight for roses too!

*   —Song of women mill workers in*
*   the 1912 Lawrence textile strike*

The history of American immigration, like most history, has generally been written by and about men. The immigrant woman tends to appear in two guises: the totally ethnocentric mainstay of the family, fighting any outside influences that might weaken her hold on her only domain, and the exploited working girl, forced by cruel economic hardship to toil in ways unsuited to "feminine nature." Popular history and literature provide only sporadic glimpses of the special bravery of women who ventured into a strange land at a time when the vast majority of immigrants were men. They were women who displayed as much courage in dangerous union struggles as they did in the dangerous childbirth of the poor, women who, as mothers, usually assumed the difficult role of mediator in the generational clashes that characterized immigrant households. Their struggles have never been adequately described.

The Italian mill women who carried banners proclaiming "We Want Bread And Roses Too" in the bitter Lawrence textile strike have occupied a smaller space in the national consciousness than immigrant girls who were forced into brothels to make a living. In reading the popular press from the turn of the century, I was struck by the amount of space devoted to the sexual exploitation of women by unscrupulous employers. I suspect that the number and sensational nature of these articles revealed more about the interests of male reporters and editors than about the most pressing hardships of immigrant life. Surely the grinding economic oppression of both male and female workers was of immeasurably greater importance than white slave rings and sexual blackmail on the job.

I have always believed that the proper place of "women's history" or "black history"—indeed, of any significant portion of human experience—is to be found not within any marginal course of minority studies but within the mainstream of scholarship and literature. The need to devise special programs in "holocaust studies" or "women's studies" is simply an admission of the failure of mainstream education to deal with important segments of history. To the extent that these programs are successful, they will self-destruct by forcing their way into the body of knowledge considered essential to anyone's education. That glorious day, however, is nowhere on the horizon.

When I began doing historical research to prepare myself for a study of contemporary immigration to the United States, I was deeply disappointed to find that the immigrant women of past generations have been neglected in books that are, in other respects, quite splendid. Irving Howe's *World of Our Fathers*, unquestionably the most comprehensive portrait of any immigrant community, is, nevertheless, a paradigm of the short shrift women receive in conventional histories. In his chapter on growing up in the ghetto, Howe includes a short special section on girls. The section is necessary because Howe's generic treatment of childhood on the Lower East Side deals entirely with boys. The experience of growing up male is the rule; growing up female is the exception. City College, the route to achievement for brilliant Jewish boys without money for tuition, deserves and gets a long section. But there were also brilliant Jewish girls who were going to Hunter College at a time when higher education for women was unheard of in most middle-class echelons of American society (much less among the poor). The sons of immigrants who went on from City College to become distinguished scientists and scholars are important figures in Howe's narrative; Nobel prize winner Rosalyn Yalow, an immigrant daughter who graduated in Hunter's first group of physics majors, is absent.

Talking about the famed Educational Alliance, Howe observed that "it was entirely possible for an immigrant father to look balefully on his son's desire to become an artist, even to think that *shmiren* pictures was a dubious or unworthy occupation, and yet want his children to learn about art, to go to museums, to try their hands at drawing, indeed, to take in 'everything.' And when the Alliance, a few blocks away, held one of its art shows displaying the work of those errant Jewish boys, this same immigrant father might venture to drop in. It didn't hurt to look."

Immigrant boys. Immigrant fathers. East European Jewish women played a more important role in encouraging the artistic and cultural pursuits of their children than women did in any immigrant community in American history (with the possible exception of the German Jews who arrived half a century earlier). Where are the immigrant daughters and mothers in Howe's descriptions of the cultural hunger of the East European Jews? And, it should be emphasized, Irving Howe is one of the most gifted and sensitive men who have chronicled immigrant cultures in the United States. Other male historians, in less encyclopedic works, have ignored women to a much greater extent.

In general, women do not loom any larger in fiction than in nonfiction accounts of the immigrant experience. There are occasional, exceptional works of fiction that do manage to illuminate the obscure figure of the immigrant wife and mother. The most notable saga of an immigrant mother by a second-generation son is Mario Puzo's *The Fortunate Pilgrim*. Puzo's descriptions of the lives of Italian women on the Lower East Side are poetic and eloquent. Here are the mothers, sitting on the stoops of their tenements:

Each in turn told a story of insolence and defiance, themselves heroic, long-suffering, the children spitting Lucifers saved by an application of Italian discipline— the razor strap or the *Tackeril*. And at the end of each story each woman recited her requiem. *Mannaggia America!*—Damn America. But in the hot summer night their voices were filled with hope, with a vigor that never sounded in their homeland. Here now was money in the bank, children who could read and write, grandchildren who would be professors if all went well. They spoke with guilty loyalty of the customs they had themselves trampled into dust.

The truth: These country women from the mountain farms of Italy, whose fathers and grandfathers had died in the same rooms in which they were born, these women loved the clashing steel and stone of the great city, the thunder of trains in the railroad yards across the street, the lights above the Palisades far across the Hudson. As children they had lived in solitude, on land so poor that people scattered themselves singly along the mountain slopes to search out a living.

Although Puzo's novel received highly favorable reviews, it was a commercial failure. Reissued in paperback after the enormous success of *The Godfather*, it continued to sell poorly. The reading public prefers the Mafia to one of the most memorable, lovingly drawn female characters in the literature of immigrant life.

Primary sources, based on the testimony of immigrant women themselves, are limited and are restricted largely to the Jewish community. Although immigrant Jews certainly did not set as high a value on education for girls as for boys, they did send their daughters to school in larger numbers—and for a longer period of time—than parents in any other immigrant group. Written, firsthand accounts by Jewish women had no counterpart in the Italian or Polish immigrant communities at the turn of the century.

Some of the most revealing accounts of everyday women's lives appeared in the *Jewish Daily Forward*'s "Bintel Brief," a column that proffered advice on everything from the desirability of piano lessons for children to the ethics of hiring maids. One letter, in 1906, came from a woman who said she was "never rich financially, but wealthy in love. I loved my husband more than anything in the world. We had seven children, the oldest is now thirteen . . . after years of hard work, my husband developed consumption . . . My husband told me he had opened a small business in Colorado, and hoped to make a living. But I heard him cough, and when I questioned him, he answered with a bitter smile that there was no cure for his illness. I immediately saw my tragedy and wouldn't let him work. I went out peddling with a basket, and left him at home with my children."

The conflict between the educational aspirations of Jewish women in the New World and the Old World tradition which defined scholarship as the realm of men was a frequent theme in letters to the *Forward*. In 1910, one woman wrote:

Since I do not want my conscience to bother me, I ask you whether a married woman has the right to go to school two evenings a week. My husband thinks I have no right to do this. . . .

Now he has announced a new decision. Because I send out the laundry to be done, it seems to him that I have too much time for myself, even enough to go to school. So from now on he will count out every penny for anything I have to buy for the house, so I will not be able to send out the laundry any more. And when I have to do the work myself there won't be any time left for such "foolishness" as going to school. I told him that I'm willing to do my own washing but that I would still be able to find time for study.

When I am alone with my thoughts, I feel I may not be right. Perhaps I should not go to school. I want to say that my husband is an intelligent man and he wanted to marry a woman who was educated. The fact that he is intelligent makes me more annoyed with him. He is in favor of the emancipation of women, yet in real life he acts contrary to his beliefs.

(The *Forward*, by the way, was on the side of the woman.)

The autobiographical novels of Anzia Yezierska, published between 1920 and 1932, are probably the most significant primary source of information about the conflict between American-educated Jewish immigrant daughters and their parents. Her most autobiographical work, *Bread Givers*, is subtitled "A struggle between a father of the Old World and a daughter of the New."

Yezierska was born in a *shtetl* in Poland in the 1880's and emigrated to America at some point during the 1890's. She was extremely well known throughout the 1920's but slipped into literary obscurity during the next decade. Her books are now enjoying a modest revival as a result of contemporary feminist interest in the hidden history of immigrant women. In her novels and short stories, Yezierska focused repeatedly on the dilemma of a woman whose intellect belonged to the New World but whose emotions belonged, at least in part, to the Old. This immigrant dilemma was not, of course, exclusively female but it was much more acute for women than for men. In *Bread Givers,* the narrator Sara Smolinsky observes:

Of course, we all knew that if God had given Mother a son, Father would have permitted a man child to share with him the best room in the house. A boy could say prayers after his father's death—that kept his father's soul alive forever. Always Father was throwing up to Mother that she had borne him no son to be an honour to his days and to say prayers for him when he died.

The prayers of daughters didn't count because God didn't listen to women. Heaven and the next world were only for men. Women could get into Heaven because they were wives and daughters of men. Women had no brains for the study of God's Torah, but they could be the servants of men who studied the Torah. Only if they cooked for the men, and washed for the men, and didn't nag or curse the men out of their homes; only if they let the men study the Torah in peace, then, maybe, they could push themselves into Heaven with the men, to wait on them there.

It is clear from this passage that Yezierska's power as a narrator is the power of an old-time war correspondent pounding out stories in a battle zone. Her works are not great literature; they are great combat dispatches. Immigrant women of her generation, who had seized freedoms undreamed-of in the world from which they came, were not sufficiently removed from the maelstrom to imbue their writing with a quality Lillian Hellman has aptly termed "a way of seeing and then seeing again." This lack of multiple perspective is characteristic of writing by first-generation immigrant men as well as women. By the second generation, though, the sons of immigrants had replaced combat reportage with a much more complex and sophisticated set of attitudes.

Where, then, were the second-generation daughters who might have provided an equally sensitive view of the world of their mothers? For the most part, they weren't writing. At the end of the 1930's, the daughters of most immigrant groups had still not achieved a status within their own ethnic communities that entitled them to complete a high school, much less a college, education. Jewish women, who had achieved a much higher educational status than the daughters of other immigrants who arrived between 1880 and 1920, were playing out the American (and the American immigrant) dream of staying home when their husbands were finally able to earn enough to support the family on one salary.

After World War II, Jewish boys became "my son/grandson, the doctor/lawyer/writer" to their immigrant parents or grandparents. Jewish girls became wives and mothers. They may have had the perspective and distance to see the immigrant experience whole, as Henry Roth and Meyer Levin and, somewhat later, Mario Puzo did. What they did not possess, as second-generation American women, was the freedom and social approval to work at recording their observations.

Third-generation women, who do possess a "social license" to write, have not chosen the immigrant experience as a major theme. That is hardly surprising; at least a generation in time and more than a generation in thought lie between women who are writing today and the immigrant grandmothers whose struggles helped form their granddaughters, the authors.

The "second-generation gap" means that a good deal of the female immigrant experience—at least the portion pertaining to the first two decades of this century—has been irretrievably lost. But immigration is a continuing phenomenon in American life, and the daughters of more recent immigrants are beginning to speak up in a society that no longer expects immigrant women to become home-bound ladies in order to fulfill the American Dream.

Maxine Hong Kingston, a Chinese-American daughter born in 1940, has written a book that combines the immediacy of Anzia Yezierska, the subtle and tender perceptions of Mario Puzo, and, last but not least, the tools of feminist analysis that were unavailable to previous generations of immigrant daughters. *The Woman*

Warrior: *Memoirs of a Girlhood Among Ghosts** makes hash of the idiotic arguments about whether there is a "special female sensibility" in literature. This memoir could only have been written by a Chinese-American woman, but its truths are no less universal because they are spoken in the voice of a doubly deprived group. (If women have been underrepresented in the literature and history of American immigration, Chinese of both sexes have been all but invisible.)

Maxine Kingston's mother, who never abandoned her Chinese name of "Brave Orchid," arrived in the United States in 1939.† The book opens with a chapter titled "No Name Woman," in which Brave Orchid tells her daughter of an aunt who drowned herself in the family well in China after giving birth to an illegitimate child.

I remember looking at your aunt one day when she and I were dressing; I had not noticed before that she had such a protruding melon of a stomach. But I did not think, "She's pregnant," until she began to look like other pregnant women, her shirt pulling and the white tops of her black pants showing. She could not have been pregnant, you see, because her husband had been gone for years. No one said anything. We did not discuss it. In early summer she was ready to have the child, long after the time when it could have been possible.

The village had also been counting. On the night the baby was to be born the villagers raided our house . . .

At first they threw mud and rocks at the house. Then they threw eggs and began slaughtering our

* Knopf, 1976.
† Kingston does not tell us, if she knows, how her mother managed to enter the country. Anti-Asian immigration laws made it almost impossible for Chinese women to immigrate to the United States between 1882 and the end of World War II. Kingston may not know how her mother managed to get here, because such secrets were closely guarded in Chinese families.

stock. We could hear the animals scream their deaths—the roosters, the pigs, a last great roar from the ox. Familiar wild heads flared in our night windows; the villagers encircled us. Some of the faces stopped to peer at us, their eyes rushing like searchlights. The hands flattened against the panes, framed heads, and left red prints . . .

The villagers pushed through both wings, even your grandparents' rooms, to find your aunt's, which was also mine until the men returned . . . They ripped up her clothes and shoes and broke her combs, grinding them underfoot. They tore her work from the loom. They scattered the cooking fire and rolled the new weaving in it. We could hear them in the kitchen breaking our bowls and banging the pots. They overturned the great waist-high earthenware jugs; duck eggs, pickled fruits, vegetables burst out and mixed in acrid torrents . . .

When they left, they took sugar and oranges to bless themselves. They cut pieces from the dead animals. Some of them took bowls that were not broken and clothes that were not torn. Afterward we swept up the rice and sewed it back up into sacks. But the smells from the spilled preserves lasted. Your aunt gave birth in the pigsty that night. The next morning when I went for the water, I found her and the baby plugging up the family well.

Don't let your father know that I told you. He denies her. Now that you have started to menstruate, what happened to her could happen to you. Don't humiliate us. You wouldn't like to be forgotten as if you had never been born. The villagers are watchful.

It should be clear, from this passage alone, that the power of *The Woman Warrior* cannot be encompassed by any of the usual "bookchat" adjectives. Kingston deals with a variety of issues that have been glossed over in the literature of immigrant women. Among the most important of these is a veiled but recurrent theme in generations of immigrant homes—the intense desire for a man child, the intense disappointment at the birth of a woman child. In China, Brave Orchid was a professionally trained midwife. She told her daughter horrifying stories of deformed babies left to die, including a particularly gruesome and haunting tale of a child born without an anus. What really haunted Maxine was the question of whether her mother had abetted the common Chinese practice of suffocating girl babies. "I hope this holeless baby proves that my mother did not prepare a box of clean ashes beside the birth bed in case of a girl. 'The midwife or a relative would take the back of a girl baby's head in her hand and turn her face into the ashes,' said my mother. 'It was very easy.' . . . To make my waking life American-normal, I turn on the lights before anything untoward makes an appearance. I push the deformed into my dreams, which are in Chinese, the language of impossible stories. Before we can leave our parents, they stuff our heads like the suitcases which they jam-pack with homemade underwear."

This passage, with its complete and subtle awareness of the contradictory pulls of two cultures, exemplifies the difference between the perceptions of the first and second generations. Anzia Yezierska, shouldering the special burdens of an immigrant woman at a time when possibilities for all women were extremely limited, could express only rage and pain in her account of women cleaning up after men who studied the Torah. There is rage in Maxine Kingston, too, but there is something else: The capacity to view both herself and her mother from a territory that does not belong exclusively to one culture or one generation. These territories are uncomfortable places for writers to live, but they are fine places for readers to visit.

Chinese, Yiddish, Italian: languages of impossible stories, languages of our ancestors in the worlds of our mothers. In one sense, *The Woman Warrior* is a sad reminder of the immense cultural loss connected with the literary and scholarly abdication of so many second-generation women in the 1930's, 40's, and 50's. In another sense, Maxine Hong Kingston points the way to a new and vibrant literature that may be expected from the daughters of immigrants who are arriving in the United States today. They still come, at least half a million a year, from Latin America and Asia and southern Europe. *This* second generation is growing up in a society that does not necessarily assume that man's experience is the rule and woman's the exception. To turn George Orwell around, one may hope that today's immigrant daughters, by controlling their present, may help recapture something of the common immigrant past—a past in which either sex may stand for the whole of humanity.

We <u>Did</u> Overcome

WHEN I WAS INVITED to deliver this year's commencement speech at my old high school in Okemos, Michigan, my pleasure was somewhat tempered by intimations of mortality. It seems that most members of the Class of 1977 were born in 1959—the year in which I entered the school. To get a better sense of my prospective audience, I phoned the senior-class president, who told me in a cheerful voice that "the big difference between my generation and yours is we're more realistic, more practical about life."

This young man's comment is not the first indication I have received that my generation—the generation that emerged from adolescence to young adulthood in the 1960's—has acquired a bad reputation or, more precisely, has become a victim of instant historical amnesia. Last year, I returned to Michigan State University (another alma mater) to participate in a panel on press coverage of urban affairs with my colleague Charlayne Hunter-Gault, a reporter for *The New York Times*. Hunter-Gault, as those of us who have not consigned yesterday's news to the memory hole know, was one of the black students who desegregated the University of Georgia in 1961. It was clear that many of the Michigan State students, black as well as white, neither recognized the name Charlayne Hunter nor had any idea of what it meant to be the first black student at a Southern university before the Old South became the New South.

One student was particularly surprised when I brought up the fact that Michigan State, while not segregated by law, was in fact a white institution at the beginning of the notorious sixties. When I attended the university between 1963 and 1965, it was not considered unusual that there were only a few hundred blacks in a student population of more than twenty-five thousand. There was only the softest whisper of scandal when a brilliant black professor left the university after finding he was unable to buy a house in the surrounding white town. This was the society bequeathed to my generation of Americans, black and white, Georgia- and New York- and Michigan-born. This, I told my student interlocutor, was the society my generation had tried to move closer to its professed ideals of justice. "You didn't get very far," the student replied. "You just did a lot of shouting."

As politicians are so fond of saying, it is time to set the record straight. The attitude of today's high school and college students toward my generation has been reinforced by a neo-conservative attack from *our* elders. Nothing attests more strongly to the painful, serious, and lasting nature of the changes that took place during the sixties than the perpetuation of a body of bitter myth about the radicalism of the young in that decade.

The neo-conservative myth states something like this: Those of us who became politically conscious in the sixties were independent of practical adult guidance and contemptuous of the values of previous generations; we were selfish, often cowardly, and unwilling to do the hard work that is the basis of all genuine social change; both our goals and our achievements were ephemeral.

In a recent article in *The New York Times Magazine* on the radical student milieu at City College in the 1930's, Irving Kristol wrote: "The radicalism of the 30's was decidedly an adult movement, in which young people were permitted to participate. . . . In contrast, the radicalism of the 60's was a generational movement, bereft of adult models and adult guidance . . . It is not, as some think, that we failed to impose our adult *beliefs* upon our children. That would be an absurd enterprise. What we failed to do is to transmit adult *values* to them . . . And precisely because we adults encouraged our 20-year-old children to be 'kids,' their rebellion so often resembled a bewildering and self-destructive tantrum."

Midge Decter, in an article adapted from her 1975 book *Liberal Parents, Radical Children*, tied up the personal and the political in one tidy indictment of the youth of the sixties. "The first thing to be observed about you," she lectured my generation, "is that, taken all together, you are more than usually incapable of facing, tolerating or withstanding difficulty of any kind. From the time of your earliest childhood, you have stood in a relation to the world that can only be characterized as a refusal to be tested. . . ."

Kristol, Decter, and other neo-conservatives make essentially the same indictment of my generation that I hear from high school and college students. The difference is that the older intellectuals ought to know better. We are far enough away from the sixties to have acquired a modicum of historical perspective, and the neo-conservative analysis does not stand up under any careful inspection.

In the first place, the word "radical" is frequently used as a meaningless catchall to describe everything from the black-power movement to the use of psychedelic drugs. The overuse and misuse of the word evoke an image distorted by the violent acts committed by fringe groups like the Weathermen in the sixties. Seen through this murky lens, a radical might be a civil-rights worker or a war protester or a bomb thrower; the confusion of violence with radicalism has frequently served as the basis for the indictment of an entire generation.

Many of the social phenomena sometimes associated with the radicalism of the sixties—the demands for more "relevant" courses and for more student participation in university policy-making are perfect examples—were in fact ephemeral disturbances. One need only look at the current return to traditional academic requirements in universities across the country to see the transitory nature of certain expressions of the campus radicalism of the sixties. These youthful demands did exert a disproportionate influence within academic communities, as they now exert a disproportionate influence on our picture of the sixties insofar as it is presented by academics and writers who were the reluctant "liberal parents" on the opposite side of the barricades from "radical children" in the universities.

Many changes in sexual and social behavior, rather than changes in political or intellectual values, created the most serious stresses in relationships between parents and their children. For parents now in their fifties, the student radicalism of the sixties is associated not with the protest marches but with the pain that ensued when a beloved child experimented with drugs or moved in with a member of the opposite sex without benefit of clergy. There is an enormous amount of personal anguish underlying many of the political indictments of the sixties.

There were, however, three genuine radical movements in the sixties—movements that fit the definition of radical as something that goes "to the root." They were the civil-rights movement, the peace (or antiwar) movement, and the women's liberation movement. Every political activist of my generation participated in at least one of these movements. For many of us, they

formed a continuum that was to become the incubator
of our adult energies.

It is necessary to begin with the civil-rights movement, because those of us who grew up in the sixties
can never forget it. The civil-rights movement was not,
of course, a "generational" phenomenon in the sense of
being cut off from the values of the past; its tactical and
philosophical debt to men like Thoreau and Gandhi is
too well known to need any recounting now. But the
civil-rights struggles of the sixties were conducted primarily by the young. Plenty of forty-year-old labor
leaders and seventy-year-old veterans of women's suffrage marches showed up for demonstrations, and there
were magnificent, enduring community leaders like the
late Fannie Lou Hamer. But the most important leaders
of the movement, like the Reverend Martin Luther
King, Jr., were in their twenties and thirties. And most
civil-rights workers—those who did the boring, backbreaking and frequently frightening tasks that made up
the assault on segregation—were in their teens or early
twenties. They never got any publicity unless they lost
their lives.

Although we were well aware of the religious and
philosophical underpinnings of the movement, our time
was devoted more to action than to intellectual dis-
course. This is probably the most important difference
between my generation and the left-wing students who
argued about Stalin and Trotsky in the thirties. Those
of us who worked to register black voters in Mississippi
during the summer of 1964 were closer in intentions—
and in our accomplishments—to the union men who
organized sitdown strikes in the thirties than we were to
Irving Kristol and his friends at City College. Between
1963 and 1966, I was in Mississippi, Alabama, Georgia, Virginia, and many other parts of the South as a
student reporter covering the activities of civil-rights
workers who were my own age. The reporters and civil-
rights workers didn't talk much about the constant danger; perhaps it would have been too difficult to go on
had we openly acknowledged our fear.

So it makes me angry when fifty- and sixty-year-olds

suggest that my generation refused to be tested or shirked its responsibilities to the rest of society. And it makes me sad when I meet twenty-year-olds who don't know the names of James Chaney, Michael Schwerner, and Andrew Goodman. None of us who were young then will ever forget the sick feeling in the pits of our stomachs when we heard the news that Chaney, a Mississippi black, and Schwerner and Goodman, whites from New York, were missing in Mississippi. We knew they were dead, long before their bodies were found in August, long before the Ku Klux Klan members who murdered them were arrested. It could have happened to any of us. No one who spent any time in Mississippi during that killing summer will ever forget how it felt riding down a highway and squeezing down on the floor in terror at the sight of every passing car. Who knew when a rifle might emerge from the window of a passing vehicle?

I thought of Schwerner, Chaney, and Goodman when the election returns began coming in last November and it became clear that a white Georgian had been elected President because millions of blacks are now registered to vote in the states of the Old Confederacy. I thought of them as I watched a recent television news feature about a young black sheriff in Alabama. The sheriff (a former civil-rights worker himself) was phoning Governor George Wallace and asking for the help of state law enforcement agencies in solving a crime. The crime happened to involve the killing of a black by another black. Time was when the state of Alabama wasn't much interested in the taking of a black life.

My generation changed that.

In analyzing the movements of the sixties, many social commentators drew a sharp distinction between the first half of the decade and the second. In spite of the trauma of President Kennedy's assassination, the images from the early sixties are mostly benevolent: black and white hands, linked; the strains of "We Shall Overcome," Martin Luther King's "I have a dream" speech. Even for those of us who were there, these images have softened, or have at least made bearable, the bone-memory of terror on the lonely highways, of firebombs, of rapes we knew about that went unreported because everyone knew that white girls had come from the North for all the sex they could get. As for the black girls—well, they were black, and raping *them* was a local tradition.

There is nothing soft or benevolent about the images from the second half of the sixties: the orange glow over the ruins of city slums; the daily dose of maiming and killing from Vietnam on the evening news; the stench of tear gas, vomit, and blood in the streets of Chicago at the 1968 Democratic Convention; crippled Vietnam veterans being beaten up for demonstrating against the war. Today there is a school of thought that attributes the ugliness of the late sixties to the difference between the discipline of the early civil-rights demonstrators and the strident anger of the antiwar protesters. This point of view ignores the extent to which the war stalled the gains of the civil-rights movement at just the point where they might have been consolidated.

I was slower than many others my age to see the connection between the civil-rights and antiwar movements. Between 1965 and 1967, I had a number of quarrels with friends who had become involved in antiwar activities. The Vietnam war, I argued, was a temporary phenomenon; the antiwar movement was diverting energies from the fight for social change in the United States; it was an elitist movement of rich white kids whose parents were able to buy them student deferments.

I don't remember exactly when I changed my mind, but I do remember why: It became clear to me that the war, not the protests against the war, was responsible for the frustration of so many bright hopes of the early sixties. At a Thanksgiving reunion with some black friends in 1967, we discussed the fact that the Vietnam war, unlike World War II, was being fought in disproportionate numbers by young men who where black and/or poor. By the time of his assassination, Martin Luther King had recognized that the war was responsible for neglect of social needs at home. Blacks of my generation, like Julian Bond, came to the realization long before the leaders of King's generation did.

The antiwar movement was even more of a generational phenomenon than the civil-rights movement. It is natural and appropriate that this should have been so; the young were doing the fighting and dying. If my generation had not resisted the war so strongly, I am convinced that the killing in Vietnam would still be going on. The Michigan State student who told me that the young people of the sixties "just did a lot of shouting" also told me he was dropping out of school for a year because he needed to earn enough money to finance his senior year. I smiled to myself. The boys of my generation were not free to drop out of school and work for a year, because they might have wound up in Vietnam before they earned enough money for another term of college.

Jimmy Carter's administration is being run by men who now say they were wrong about the Vietnam war. My generation was, if not right from the start, right a lot earlier.

As a writer, I take a special pride in the youthful survivors of the war who refuse to let us forget what happened to them. Neo-conservatives who consider the anti-war movement to have been a convenient excuse for reluctance to serve in the Army will not find support in Ron Kovic's book, *Born on the Fourth of July*. Kovic, who turned thirty years old on the day the Tall Ships sailed into New York harbor to celebrate the Bicentennial, did not have the luxury, as I did, of making slow decisions about the war at a safe distance. Wounded and paralyzed from the chest down, he returned from Vietnam and became active in the peace movement. His book should be required reading for anyone who thinks the antiwar movement was a lark.

It is no accident that so many female veterans of the civil-rights movement and the antiwar movement ultimately became involved in the women's liberation movement. The attitude toward women embodied in Stokely Carmichael's famous remark—"The only position for women in our movement is prone"—was only one reason why so many of us decided to start fighting the bigotry that was directed against our sex rather than the color of our skin. The most important lesson we learned from both the civil-rights and antiwar movements was that no one was going to fight for us until we started fighting for ourselves.

Before I graduated from college in 1965, I made a trip to Detroit for a job interview at a newspaper that had been printing my articles for years. The managing editor was eager to hire me and said he was sure I would enjoy working for the society page. He explained that it was the policy of the paper to hire women for the women's page, because Detroit was a dangerous city and it wouldn't do to have women covering stories there at night.

In that moment, I realized that—for all my involvement in civil rights—I had never fully understood what prejudice and discrimination were. When I returned to the campus to lick my wounds before setting up more job interviews, a black professor said, "Well, you may want to start up a new branch of the civil-rights movement." The remark stayed with me.

I recently received a Michigan State alumni bulletin featuring a pretty young woman who had just been named a Rhodes scholar. She said she believed in equal opportunity but was unwilling to identify with the sillier aspects of the feminist movement. She was happy, she said, to be considered a member of "mankind."

I wish this young lady nothing but the best and would certainly not quarrel with her happiness at being a member of mankind. However, the happiness of being a Rhodes scholar would not be hers without the feminist movement. When I was in college, only men were eligible for Rhodes scholarships.

Those of us who were formed by the radical movements of the sixties would not have it any other way. We don't want anyone, black or white, to have to die for the right to cast a ballot. We don't want our younger brothers to die or be crippled in a senseless war. We don't want our youthful sisters to lose—or, worse yet, to fail to try for—scholarships or jobs simply because they were born female. But it would be nice if the current crop of high school and college students realized that the generation now in its thirties helped free the energies of today's youth for other battles—or, at least, for the next stage of the old battles.

And it is time for our own parents to see the radicalism of the sixties for what it was: not a self-indulgent temper tantrum but a series of movements which—however painful and disturbing it may have been—addressed itself to fundamental injustices affecting Americans of all ages.

—April 1977

The Education of a Feminist: Part One

The problem lay buried, unspoken, for many years in the minds of American women. It was a strange stirring, a sense of dissatisfaction, a yearning that women suffered in the middle of the twentieth century in the United States. Each suburban wife struggled with it alone. As she made beds, shopped for groceries, matched slip-cover material, ate peanut butter sandwiches with her children, chauffeured Cub Scouts and Brownies, lay beside her husband at night—she was afraid to ask even of herself the silent question—"Is this all?"

The opening lines of *The Feminine Mystique* did not, I confess, grip the imagination of a nineteen-year-old "comp lit" student with the familiar lyricism of "it was the best of times, it was the worst of times"; the appealing, if cockeyed, certainty that "happy families are all alike," or the blunt force of "I am an American,

Chicago-born." Nor did they fit into an intellectual framework that was being formed not only by an eccentric, self-selected course of fiction (Michigan State University, in 1964, gave its honor students complete freedom to avoid a well-rounded education if they would only read *something* and pay no attention to the rumbles of discontent being heard from a far-off place called Berkeley) but by the more predictable collegiate influences of Freud, Marx, Hegel, Kant, *et al*.

Nevertheless, it was Betty Friedan's book (not, of course, recommended or required for any college course) which initiated a slow intellectual process that was to change my mind and my life. It has been just fifteen years since I picked up a copy of the first paperback edition of *The Feminine Mystique*; in this short epoch, as epochs go, modern feminism has become a movement with so many powerful political and emotional implications that many Americans have forgotten, if they ever knew, about the intellectual void that had to be filled before a "women's movement" could exist.

The tumultuous activism of the movement is not the only factor that has obscured the intellectual foundations of contemporary feminism. It has become unfashionable to speak of intellectualism with respect in almost any context. The very word "intellectual," battered from the left and from the right (remember *The Greening of America* on one hand and the collected speeches of Spiro Agnew on the other), has acquired fusty, pejorative connotations. The Oxford English Dictionary's definition of an intellectual as an "enlightened person" is no longer in favor, even among people who would at one time have been proud to consider themselves intellectuals. At best, the once-honorable word conjures up visions of an owlish, irrelevant, hopelessly *middle-class* professor entombed by a wall of books. Many feminists, stung by charges that the movement is meaningful only to middle-class women, are particularly uneasy about the intellectual (and social) origins of the current wave of feminism. But the fact is plain: The unfinished feminist revolution began—though it has not ended—with a book written by a privileged middle-class woman who had enjoyed the benefits of an elite education (in contrast to other modern revolutions, which began with books written by privileged middle-class men).

The dog-eared pages of my old copy of *The Feminine Mystique* are smeared with dried ketchup stains and undergraduate exclamation points in the margins—testimony to the fact that the book was well read. I look at those pages, and I have no trouble remembering my excitement at the title of the first chapter: "The Problem That Has No Name." Not that a light bulb flashed on over my head in comic-strip fashion; it took some years for me to realize that feminism might be as valuable an intellectual tool as any other set of ideas. But I recognized the problem that had no name—right from the start. I had grown up with it, but what is one to do or think about a "problem" that lacks a definition?

It is difficult to describe, without seeming to exaggerate, the condition of anger and bewilderment that was the lot of a bright, ambitious girl growing up in an ordinary American town, receiving an ordinary American education, in the 1950's. I stress the word "ordinary." It is no accident that most leaders and theoreticians of the feminist movement either grew up in the large cities that are the centers of culture in the United States or were educated at the old Eastern women's colleges which, whatever their deficiencies, had the singular virtue of exposing young women to a concentration of brilliant female minds not to be found in other American institutions.*

* The chief drawback of these institutions, before most of them shifted to co-education in the late 1960's, was hopelessly entangled with their major asset. Surrounded by extremely bright young women as classmates, encouraged to express themselves by the presence of so many accomplished older women, the graduates of these prestigious colleges went out into the world with almost no experience of speaking up in front of or competing with men. Given the outstanding intellectual qualifications and privileged economic backgrounds of so many of the students, the surprising fact is not that the Seven Sisters produced so many women leaders but that they produced so few.

Again, I stress the ordinariness of the environment in which I lived until, at age twenty, I went forth to pursue the fantasies of newspaper reporting inspired by the first movie version of *The Front Page*. Lansing, Michigan, is neither the center of the universe nor a backward hamlet. When I was a girl, Lansing was a city of more than 100,000 people—then, as now, the capital of the state, headquarters of the Oldsmobile division of General Motors, and home of Michigan State University. My family lived in Okemos, a suburb of professors, businessmen, and civil servants who had scraped up enough money to move out of the aging central city. Named after the last Indian chief who inhabited the area, Okemos was separated into what the realtors called "subdivisions": Indian Hills, Chippewa Hills, Tacoma Hills, Ottawa Hills, Forest Hills and—an afterthought—Hiawatha Park. We lived in Forest Hills, which was neither the richest nor the poorest of the subdivisions. A few of the rich kids, who lived in Tacoma Hills and Indian Hills, had swimming pools. The poorer kids, in Ottawa Hills and Chippewa Hills, had to share bedrooms with brothers and sisters. We Forest Hills kids had our own bedrooms but no pools in the back yard.

In this middle-class milieu, the only working women I knew were grade school or high school teachers. Until I graduated from college, I had *never* known a woman who did anything else—no women doctors, lawyers, journalists, or veterinarians—no secretaries or waitresses or cooks, either. Of course, I was aware that a great many women did secretarial work, but I assumed that they were young and waiting to catch a husband or unlucky enough to be divorced. Only one of my friends had a working mother, and she was a first-grade teacher. Another friend had a mother who, it was said, had been a researcher for *Time* magazine before she came home to Michigan to marry a doctor. My own mother did not have a job, and she made it clear that the "wildness" of a few kids in the neighborhood—those who turned their record players up too loud and rode their bikes across the neighbors' lawns—was attributable to the fact that they had mothers who "worked." I had no way of checking out this information, because I didn't know the wild kids or their mothers. To this day, I don't know whether they were real people or whether, in my mother's mythology, they occupied the position of Sophie Portnoy's errant neighbor, the one who was responsible for her son's colitis because she gadded about in the local stores and failed to prevent her little boy from eating hot dogs and doughnuts in greasy spoons.

So the only women I knew when I was growing up were housewives. And there I was, wanting to be "a writer" from the age of eleven (when I gave up the impractical dream of becoming a baseball player). I didn't want to be a housewife; I had taken note of The Problem That Had No Name before Betty Friedan named it, but I had no frame of reference to make sense out of what I saw. I didn't know any women who worked, but I knew women who drank. And women who took barbiturates. And women who slept the day away, still in their nightgowns when their children returned home after school. One Friday afternoon, I went home with a girlfriend to spend the night and we found her mother staring glassy-eyed into an empty bottle of Scotch. "Mom, you promised not to do that any more," my friend said. "It's because you don't have a date for the dance tonight," Mom replied. Then, turning to me, "And you, Susan, you don't have a date either. Your mother must feel terrible too."

It has been suggested, by women as well as men, that the hindsight of feminist conviction has cast the lives of the women of my childhood in a worse light than they could have appeared to me at the time. Not so. Only since the feminist movement have I been able to bring any understanding to bear on the question of why those suburban women locked themselves into, or permitted themselves to be locked into, what seemed to me such a stultifying existence. My mother, who found herself a job after my younger brother entered college, has told me she now feels that she and our entire family would have been better off if she had gone to work much earlier. "In those days," she said, "it wasn't even a question you could ask yourself—whether you'd be better off, even whether you might be a better mother, if you had real interests outside of your home."

That my mother's repressed questions might be related to my own limitless ambitions was not something that could have occurred to me when I was a teen-ager. I only knew, by age fifteen, that I had a boundless contempt for women who wrote "Occupation: Housewife" on the census form. The conclusion I drew, from the narrow vision of my girlfriends as well as from their mothers' lives, was that women were, as a group, quite stupid. *I*, of course, was an exception. In high school and college, I was often told that I thought and/or wrote like a man, and I was always pleased to hear it. If this sounds like an emotional rather than an intellectual conundrum, I can only say I did not see it that way at the time. The one question that bothered me was why other women were so dumb.

I was a pushy, nervy, hard-working kid, and everything conspired to reinforce my thinking. When a high school counselor suggested that I major in education because I would make an excellent English teacher and teaching was always a good fall-back position for a woman, I snorted and paid no attention: The counselor was a woman, and I took her advice as one more proof of female stupidity. In my senior year, I became the first girl to win a college scholarship from the local chapter of Sigma Delta Chi (then an all-male journalism fraternity, now just another coed organization). The award was presented by Helen Thomas, then a junior White House correspondent for United Press International. Thomas was, as it happened, the first female reporter I had ever met, but she was also an example of what I did not want to become. Now a respected senior political correspondent, Thomas was, in 1963, assigned chiefly to stories about Jackie, John-John, and Caroline Kennedy, and Caroline's pony, Macaroni. No doubt she could have told me some interesting stories about what it was really like, being a woman in a man's world. But she didn't tell any tales and I certainly didn't ask for any. The race, as far as I was concerned, was still to the swift.

So I moved fifteen minutes away from home to Michigan State University, an institution of twenty-six thousand students, give or take a few hundred. All of my professors were men. At a university of that size, there must have been a few women faculty members, but I didn't run into any of them—either as a student or a reporter for the campus newspaper.

One of my professors, a journalism instructor who was in fact the only good teacher of English composition at the university, did me the invaluable favor of suggesting that I might just find the going a little harder in my chosen profession because I was a woman. Naïve as it may have been for someone who thought she was so smart, I had simply never considered the possibility that I might be defeated in anything that mattered to me. I already had a plan: I would get a job as a reporter for a big-city newspaper and support myself until, like Twain and Hemingway, I was ready to forsake the transitory excitement of news in order to produce masterpieces of fiction. My professor pointed out that newspapers were not as eager to hire young women as young men, because they were afraid the women would quit work as soon as they got married and had children. Therefore, he admonished, I must have a thick collection of professional clippings when it came time to apply for a job. He too had a plan: His best student was graduating and leaving a job as a campus "stringer" for *The Detroit Free Press*. I would be good at the job and the professor would recommend me. A university the size of Michigan State is an important source of news; at eighteen, my byline began appearing regularly over prominently displayed stories in the second largest newspaper in the state.

Why, in the course of these triumphs, was I bothered enough about the "woman question" to pick up a copy of *The Feminine Mystique*? My interest was due in part to the education I was getting and in part to the education I was not getting. I had heard enough about Freud in Psych. 101 to make me want to read more of him. It didn't make any sense to me, a theory of feminine nature based entirely on the behavior of patients in nineteenth-century Vienna. If Freud was to be believed, most of what I wanted in life was perfectly normal for a man and perfectly crazy for a woman.

But it was literature, not psychiatry (a discipline bearing much too marked a resemblance to religion to have a significant impact on a nineteen-year-old agnostic) which posed a genuinely serious and troubling intellectual problem. It had begun to dawn on me that the statement "you write like a man" was not an unmixed compliment. How could I "write like a man" when I was a woman, albeit an odd sort of woman by most people's definitions (my own included)? By 1964, the mid-point of my college years, I had read only two books by women regarded as important writers—the painfully dull *Silas Marner* and *Jane Eyre*. A partial list of the writers I had not read (most of whose names I did not even know at the time) should suffice: Jane Austen, Simone de Beauvoir, the Brontë sisters (*Jane Eyre* excepted), Willa Cather, Colette, Carson McCullers, Doris Lessing, Flannery O'Connor, George Sand, Eudora Welty, Edith Wharton.

A lousy education? Perhaps. Certainly, I never could have gotten a diploma from Radcliffe or Sarah Lawrence without having read Jane Austen. Nevertheless, my literary education, acquired on my own as well as through the admittedly minimal demands of Michigan State, was considerably more advanced than that of most American college students. Ignorant as I was of writing by women, I was well versed in the works of male major writers. Dostoevsky, Tolstoy, Chekhov, Turgenev, Flaubert, Proust, Dickens, Hardy, Faulkner, James: I had read them all. And, because I could never control the habit of reading for pleasure even while I was limping toward a college degree, I was even familiar with books by living writers. Saul Bellow and Philip Roth (neither of whom appeared in my *goyische* lit courses) were my favorites. I remember reading Roth's brilliant short story "Defender of the Faith" and wishing (a) that I had written it myself or (b) that some woman would publish a short story of that high caliber in a women's magazine. But that was silly. Literary quality and "women's magazine" offered a contradiction in terms.

I recently read a passage from a 1960 *Ladies' Home Journal* (cited in *The Feminine Mystique*) to a twenty-one-year-old woman I know. She laughed and laughed and refused to believe that such an article had ever been published. The passage described the happy life of a Texas housewife named Janice in a regular feature called "How America Lives."

Sometimes, she washes and dries her hair before sitting down at a bridge table at 1:30. Mornings she is having bridge at her house are the busiest, for then she must get out the tables, cards, tallies, prepare fresh coffee and organize lunch . . . During the winter months, she may play as often as four days a week from 9:30 to 3 p.m. . . . Janice is careful to be home before her sons return from school at 4 p.m.

She is not frustrated, this new young housewife. An honor student at high school, married at eighteen, remarried and pregnant at twenty, she has the house she spent seven years dreaming and planning in detail. She is proud of her efficiency as a housewife, getting it all done by 8:30 . . .

"I love my home," she says . . . The pale gray paint in her L-shaped living and dining room is five years old, but still in perfect condition . . . The pale peach and yellow and aqua damask upholstery looks spotless after eight years' wear. "Sometimes I feel I'm too passive, too content," remarks Janice, fondly regarding the wristband of large family diamonds she wears even when the watch itself is being repaired . . . Her favorite possession is her four-poster spool bed with a pink taffeta canopy. "I feel just like Queen Elizabeth sleeping in that bed," she says happily. (Her husband sleeps in another room, since he snores.)

"I'm so grateful for my blessings," she says. "Wonderful husband, handsome sons with dispositions to match, big comfortable house . . . I'm thankful for my good health and faith in God and such material possessions as two cars, two TV's and two fireplaces."

The inability of a twenty-one-year-old to see such a passage as anything other than a parody is a tribute to the profound changes in thought and behavior that have taken place during the past fifteen years. It is difficult to explain to anyone under the age of twenty-five what feminism meant to women of my generation, reared at the height of the "back to the home" movement after the Second World War.

During the first year of my feminist education, which began on the spring day in 1964 when I bought a copy of *The Feminine Mystique*, I learned a variety of amazing things:

1. There was indeed a "back to the home" movement after the war—a movement which wiped out many of the educational and professional gains women had made in the 1920's, 30's, and early 40's. Women's magazines in the 30's and early 40's had published serious fiction and non-fiction, by male and female authors, instead of the drivel exemplified by "How America Lives."

2. There was an alternative—in fact, there were many alternatives—to the Freudian view of feminine nature and feminine sexuality.

3. Contrary to what I had heard in school, the nineteenth-century feminists were not a bunch of loony, frustrated hags. Their thoughts were worth reading. (At the time, Susan B. Anthony was the only "suffragette" whose name I knew. In the history textbook my school had used, the women's suffrage movement occupied half a paragraph.)

4. The educational system was geared to discourage girls from pursuing serious "masculine" goals. Stupidity was not an adequate explanation of why so many counselors encouraged girls to teach elementary school and why so many girls faithfully followed their advice.

5. There was a body of great literature by women. I knew nothing about it.

Again, there are those who would contend that my

ignorance was the result of a particularly horrible education. Again, I say I had an education that was, in some respects, better than average. Insofar as the history of women was concerned, it was certainly no worse than the American norm.

Imagine the heady discoveries of 1964! Emily Dickinson was not, it seemed, a saccharine nature poet. But wasn't she a hermit, a complete weirdo, like all great women who "wrote"? Perhaps she was, but there were others who weren't—women who, in much harder times, insisted on their right to both love and work. George Sand. Colette. Margaret Fuller. Anna Akhmatova (a spur to learn Russian). During that year, I encountered the idea that it was not necessary to deny I was a woman like other women in order to become a person of worldly achievement. I greeted this idea with a good deal of suspicion and was unable to absorb it emotionally for many years. One does not lightly cast off habits of the mind that have been extremely useful in the past; the idea that I had nothing in common with other dumb women had played no small role in helping me avoid snares ranging from the bad advice of school counselors to the accidental teen-age pregnancies that aborted the development of so many of the girls I knew.

But I was one of the lucky ones. My feminist education began just before life handed me an unforgettable (unforgettable only because it was the first) setback based solely on the fact that I was, in the end, only a woman. I had intended, logically enough, to go to work for *The Detroit Free Press* after I graduated in the summer of 1965. In January, I showed up for a job interview that I thought was only a formality. I had, after all, been writing for the paper for two years. The editor greeted me cheerfully, told me how happy he would be to have me working full time for the paper, and started describing the duties of a society reporter. "*Society* reporter." I gulped. He explained that I would start by writing up weddings but, with my demonstrated talent, I would soon progress to writing feature articles about women's charities and child care. I had assumed, I said, that I would be hired for general assignment since that was what I had been doing in Lansing. No, he answered, the paper never hired women for anything but society news. Women couldn't be hired for general assignment, because it was too dangerous to send women out on night stories.

Believe it or not, this was the first indication I had ever received that anything more than talent and hard work was required for success. Thanks to the beginnings of feminism in my own mind, I was able to understand that the editor was part of the same system as my high school counselor. For years, I had been fighting a battle to prove to myself and everyone else that I was not just a girl. I now began to see that the battle should be fought against the system and not against myself.

A month after the debacle at the *Free Press*, I had almost slid all the way back into my former state of innocent arrogance when the city editor of *The Washington Post* extended his hand after a fifteen-minute interview and said I was hired—for general assignment. *He* wasn't concerned about sending me out on assignment at night, and the *Post* was a much better paper than the *Free Press*. Perhaps the "woman problem" had reared its head for the last time.

On the way out of the building, I had to stop by the personnel department to fill out forms and take routine tests required of every new employee. Part of the test was a five-hundred-word essay. The personnel director assigned me the topic: "How I Plan to Combine Being a Career Woman and a Wife."

So the problem wasn't going to go away. But at least it was no longer a Problem That Had No Name.

—September 1978